Test Your Child:
Birth to 6

Test Your Child: Birth to 6

Jeanmarie Pehl Scarr
Judy K. Werder Sargent, Ph.D.

Camino Books, Inc.
Philadelphia

Manufactured in the United States of America

Library of Congress Cataloging-in-Publication Data

Pehl, Jeanmarie Scarr, 1956-
    Test Your Child: Birth to 6 / Jeanmarie Pehl Scarr & Judy K. Werder Sargent.
    Includes bibliographical references and index.
    ISBN 0-940159-28-7 (Paper: alk. paper)   ᵛᵇᵇ
    1. Child   development—Testing   I.   Sargent,   Judy   K.   Werder,
    1949-   II. Title
RJ51.D48P44   1995   95-14755
305.23'1'0287—dc20

Disclosure Statement

Certain cautions must be noted to avoid misinterpretations from the results of the checklist. The information derived from the checklist indicates how your child's development generally compares to other children his or her age. Results should not be used to identify children who may later demonstrate school-related problems. *Test Your Child: Birth to 6* is not a diagnostic test instrument. It is not designed to diagnose learning disabilities, physical illnesses, psychological disorders, speech defects, or social and behavioral dysfunctions. This book is a parent's guide. It is designed to shed light on your observations and enhance your understanding of and relationship with your child. Results from the checklist can help your pediatrician perform detailed professional diagnostic assessment, if needed.

This book is available at a special discount on bulk purchases for promotional, business and educational use.

For information, write to:

Publisher
Camino Books
P.O. Box 59026
Philadelphia, PA 19102

For John, Michael, and all the children
who inspired these pages,
and
in loving memory
of our littlest angel, Thomas Scarr.

Contents

Foreword

The developmental assessment of children is a major concern of pediatricians and primary care physicians. Parents are not usually precise historians and when asked specific details about their child's development, the parents' responses are often vague and inaccurate. In most instances, exact information is not germane to the situation presented to the doctor. However, if there is any doubt about a child's neuropsychological development, details pertaining to the attainment of specific milestones become important in the overall assessment of the youngster in question.

Many who are parents for the first time are compulsive about "filling in the blanks" outlined in various parenting books and will keep up with the documentation of important events in a child's life. Often as the child gets older, when both parents work, or when a second or third child enters the family, record-keeping becomes a low-priority item and is either incomplete or is simply not done at all.

Although *Test Your Child: Birth to 6* is a record book for parents, it is much different from the others. It is extremely easy to use. One need only place a checkmark in the appropriate column and record the month. Also, this book serves as a reminder to parents to schedule appropriate visits to their child's physician. The book stresses the proper times for immunizations on a schedule that has been developed by the American Academy of Pediatrics. In addition, *Test Your Child: Birth to 6* provides parents with information that is useful for stimulating their child's physical, social and intellectual development. The book reinforces parenting with suggestions such as reading and singing to your child. Anticipatory guidance is featured, such as informing parents of safety measures in handling their child, preventing injuries, and insuring a safe environment. Sound advice is given on the immediate management of emergencies and when parents should call their physician.

Test Your Child: Birth to 6 is an excellent manual that can be used not only in tracking a child's development, but as a resource to parents in childrearing methods. It provides a wealth of information regarding child care that will supplement the professional care provided by the child's doctor. This book can also prove beneficial to the child's physician by allowing easy and rapid access to important information in the areas of movement, growing, communication, relating to others, thinking and adapting.

Test Your Child: Birth to 6 is a single publication that can replace many of the popular books written on the important responsibility of raising a child.

> Patrick S. Pasquariello, Jr., M.D.
> Director, Diagnostic Center
> The Children's Hospital of Philadelphia
> Professor of Pediatrics,
> The University of Pennsylvania
> School of Medicine

Introduction

From birth to 6 years old, a child develops in wondrous ways. As parents, we watch in amazement as our children learn to walk, to think, to talk, to play, and to become independent. A child who is healthy physically, emotionally, and mentally is the hope of every parent. The magical growth that occurs in the early months and years forms the foundation for the child's personality, talents, and abilities that will be carried forward into life's experiences. A child who develops normally in early childhood has a smooth transition to school years.

But just how do parents really know if their child is developing normally? New parents don't really have a clue unless they are willing to delve into early childhood literature. For experienced parents, instinct and observation offer insight into whether or not the second or third child's development is on track. But because each child develops uniquely, even experienced parents have cause to wonder about their child's development.

The Importance of Developmental Milestones

Milestones are those behaviors that are the major markers of development and growth. Parents need a measuring stick against which to evaluate their child's progress along the milestones. *Test Your Child: Birth to 6* is a guided observation tool. It is designed to make that appraisal process simple and revealing. This easy-to-use guidebook provides a way of evaluating where your child is in terms of her early childhood development. It shows whether your child is developing normally for her age, is emerging toward the next developmental level, or shows developmentally advanced or delayed behaviors.

Knowledge of your child's current developmental stage as compared to the milestones in this guidebook helps you communicate with others important in your child's early years—like doctors, teachers, babysitters, and relatives. Understanding your child's developmental strengths and weaknesses helps you plan better for your child's needs.

Using *Test Your Child: Birth to 6* will give you information and confidence when communicating with others. You will be able to assure well-meaning friends and others that your child is developing appropriately and ignore bad advice with confidence.

About the *Test Your Child: Birth to 6* Milestones

The milestones included in this guidebook have been carefully developed from thousands of researched behaviors observed by the most renowned child development experts—all compiled and simplified into a convenient format that is easy for you to use.

Each of the resources listed in the reference section at the end of this book reflects the research findings of noted professionals in the fields of pediatrics, education, child development, and psychology. The infant and early childhood behaviors cited in these findings were catalogued, categorized, and cross-validated. Results of this cross-validation revealed the most supported and readily observable behaviors at each age level.

The *Test Your Child: Birth to 6* milestones were developed from these highly established and validated markers of early childhood growth and development. Each of the five selected milestones in each age category was carefully phrased in simple, easy-to-understand language. The Appendix at the end of this book offers further explanation of each milestone.

How Your Child Develops

It's important to realize that although children have unique differences, the developmental phases a normal child experiences are the same from child to child. Children all experience the same milestones and sequences, but will differ in their individual styles and rates of development. From birth, you watch as your child begins to move, communicate, relate, think, adapt, and grow. These aspects of growth are all marvelously intertwined in your child's development. In *Test Your Child: Birth to 6*, we have separated these facets to help you focus on and observe the key milestones involved in each area of development. This guidebook is organized into six sections—Moving, Communicating, Relating, Thinking, Adapting, and Growing, all in a checklist format for you to follow.

- *Moving* includes the physical skills your child develops in order to move about safely and independently in her environment.
- *Communicating* evolves as your child learns to listen and understand others, while beginning to express herself.
- *Relating* includes the social and emotional milestones encountered in establishing relationships with others.
- *Thinking* involves those observable behaviors that reflect your child's growing intellect and ability to think and solve problems.
- *Adapting* includes all those basic skills—like eating, dressing, and toileting—needed for your child to become independent.
- *Growing* involves the facets of physical development usually monitored by your child's health care providers—nurses, doctors, and dentists.

How to Observe Your Child's Development

As the parent, you are the expert. You are more knowledgeable about your child than anyone. Every day, you are naturally observing your child's development. *Test Your Child: Birth to 6* will help you focus and record your observations. What you see, hear, and notice about how your child grows and interacts with her environment will be organized in a way to help you plan for your child's future.

To begin to use the guidebook, flip through the pages and notice the six sections—Moving, Communicating, Relating, Thinking, Adapting, and Growing. Each section begins with a brief introduction that provides basic information about each aspect of development and describes specific ways to observe your child's behavior in a natural way. Skim through the behaviors listed in the guidebook, and note that they are written in brief, simple statements. Use these statements to help you visualize what you will be looking for. For a more complete explanation of each behavior, refer to the Appendix in the back of this book. Note that the behaviors are organized by age from birth to 72 months.

You will be looking for these behaviors in your child. You might want to choose one day to pay particular attention to the milestones in just one category. It's a good idea to read through the milestones you will be observing and recording. Then move through the day's normal activities, keeping *Test Your Child: Birth to 6* close at hand, and watch your child with those specific behaviors in mind. Allow your child many opportunities to show these behaviors naturally.

Using *Test Your Child: Birth to 6* for Your Child

Read through the milestones listed in the categories of *Test Your Child: Birth to 6* that you plan to observe. If you are not sure what to look for, refer to the Appendix for further explanation.

To the right of each item, you have the option to check "No," "Almost," or "Yes." Note the child's age at the time of observation next to your checkmark. You may even want to make notations as you observe (see the example below).

Sample:
5-8 MONTHS

	NO age ✓	ALMOST age ✓	YES age ✓
Creeps, crawls, or otherwise moves about.	_____	_____	_____
Passes a toy from one hand to the other.	_____	_____	_____
Pulls self to standing.	_____	_____	_____
Picks up small toys with fingertips.	_____	_____	_____
Makes walking motion when held.	_____	_____	_____

If you observed a behavior sometime before, but you don't remember exactly when, just check "Yes" without recording the age. If you are simply not sure, just leave the item blank and record a question mark next to the item. You can help create a situation to aid your observation. For example, you can put an enticing object out of reach, or you can say to your child, "Can you stand on one foot like this?"

Begin at an age level below your child's current age. For example, if your child is 6 months old, begin with the items for the 0 to 4 month level. You do not have to be watching your child when you record items in the guidebook, but you should be certain of your child's performance on a behavior before you check it.

Continue checking behaviors until you are checking mostly "No"'s. In fact, when you have checked "No" for all five behaviors at an age level, stop recording, and realize that these are your child's next developmental steps.

After completing the checklist, look back at the pattern of checkmarks and note whether your child is generally at her level, is behind her level, or is showing behavior ahead of her level. If you see a puzzling pattern of "No"'s or "Almost"'s checked, go back and read the items again. Then refer to the detailed descriptions in the Appendix to be sure you understand the behavior. Be sure your child is not resisting your attempts at observing her. When this happens, try to watch her during more natural activities and situations. After these adjustments, go back and recheck your observations.

The more familiar you are with the behaviors in *Test Your Child: Birth to 6*, the easier it will be for you to keep your record up-to-date. Think of many ways and situations where your child would naturally use the skill and expose your child to these situations. Note that you should be sure to observe across all six categories to gain a complete picture of your child's development.

We recommend that you complete all six sections of the guidebook in more than one session or over several days. It might be more convenient for you to allow a week or so to complete all six sections.

Use *Test Your Child: Birth to 6* to observe your child regularly—for example, every 4 months through the first 2 years, then every 6 months through age 4, then every 12 months until she is 6 years old. For each subsequent observation, recheck every behavior previously marked as a "No" or "Almost." Simply record a check (✓) for "Yes," and indicate the age when these behaviors are finally accomplished.

Enriching Your Child's Development

As you spend time with your child, praise and make little suggestions that will lead to her success. For example, say, "You did it! Now try this." Don't offer rewards or force your child to do something she just doesn't want to do.

Remember that when your child refuses an activity in the morning, it doesn't mean she won't show interest later in the day, so you may want to try it another time. Major theorists agree that a parent can't push or force development in children, but they can provide opportunity and environment. Create a rich world of exploration for your child. Regardless of her chronological age, present inviting opportunities for your child to experiment with behaviors she may not have previously attempted. Provide an emotionally comfortable environment for your child to practice her emerging skills.

When to be Concerned and What to Do

Certainly do be concerned if your child is behind her age level in a category—that is, if she has all "No"'s for the behaviors below her current age level. Don't be concerned, however, if your child has not accomplished all five behaviors in her current age level.

Look for missing steps within each category and introduce your child to a myriad of activities that will allow her to practice the skill needed to accomplish a step.

Any concerns should be discussed with your pediatrician and with others experienced in child development. Remember, however, that you are the consistent observer in your child's development. Combine all the information you have learned from the experts with all of your observations recorded and organized in *Test Your Child: Birth to 6*. If you are still concerned, study additional material about your specific concerns. You may use the reference section in this book to help you get started; we found that these experts offered considerable insight and useful information about child development.

Remember that this guidebook is developed from the thousands of behaviors reported by renowned child development experts. You should feel confident using your recordings in *Test Your Child: Birth to 6* as a basis for discussing your concerns with your pediatrician, your child's teachers, and professional evaluators.

PART 1

The Checklist

1

The Checklist for Moving

Moving about is natural and is one of your child's first mechanisms for learning. During the early months, your child's motor development becomes the window through which you observe her overall development.

Moving includes the physical skills your child develops in order to move about safely and independently in her environment. Motor development, expressed as moving, helps your child develop an understanding of the important concepts of space, time, and direction needed in all aspects of development.

A feeling of independence and self-pride comes from being able to locomote (to crawl, creep, and walk). As your child becomes better able to master her environment, her self-confidence is enhanced. Movement allows the child a way to actively attack a problem, which consequently leads to a sense of accomplishment. By promoting physical control, movement contributes to school success. It allows the child to fully develop an awareness of left and right needed for reading and for following all sorts of directions.

Your Child's Motor Development

Children follow the same milestones and sequences in motor development, regardless of physical differences. As they move in their environment, their individual rates and styles of moving are unique.

Large muscle actions like those needed for sitting, standing, walking and jumping develop earlier than small muscle actions like writing or eating with a spoon. Underlying the ability to move successfully are the skills of balance, strength, flexibility, and coordination, all of which develop naturally as your child explores her world.

How to Observe Your Child Moving

Pay attention to your child's movements. Put your infant on the floor and, from all angles, watch her move. Scatter interesting toys about and watch how your child moves in reaction to the toys. Provide a safe environment for your growing child to crawl, walk, jump, climb, balance, and run. Watch your child's movements as she plays alone and with others. Do guard your child's safety as you are watching her move about, while promoting her sense of independence. For example, walk or stand near your child as she begins to use the stairs.

Completing the Moving Section

Read through the *Moving* items from beginning to end. Use the statements to help you visualize the kinds of movements to watch, and refer to the Appendix for further explanation. As you familiarize yourself with the *Moving* behaviors, think about different situations where your child would naturally show those behaviors. Prepare to provide those opportunities for your child to aid your observations and her development. Follow the guidelines in the Introduction for recording your observations.

Enriching Your Child's Motor Development

Create an environment that allows your child to have thousands of little victories and successes every day. Allow your child, from the time she is a very young infant, to move on her own. Avoid holding or carrying your child constantly. The best way to promote motor development is to let your infant move about naturally. During the first year, place a blanket on the floor and let your child roll about and experiment with manipulating toys as well as her own body.

Provide opportunities and time for your child to be challenged at her developmental level, not necessarily her age. Let her try new ways of moving, and encourage her to do things for herself. Doing things for your child leads her to believe that she is incapable and can diminish her self-confidence.

Encourage climbing, running, jumping, throwing, bending, twisting, rolling, balancing, turning, and batting. Praise and comment by making little suggestions that will lead to successes. For example, say "Try to swing your arms when you jump," or "I wonder what would happen if you . . ."

The more your child moves, the better she will become at moving. Most of all, your child's movement experiences should be natural and enjoyable.

Moving

0-4 MONTHS

	NO age ✓	ALMOST age ✓	YES age ✓
Holds head up for 10 or more seconds			
Reaches and grabs a toy.			
Rolls over.			
Sits steadily when held.			
Pushes up on arms.			

5-8 MONTHS

Creeps, crawls, or otherwise moves about.			
Passes a toy from one hand to the other.			
Pulls self to standing.			
Picks up small toys with fingertips.			
Makes walking motion when held.			

9-12 MONTHS

Creeps or crawls up two or more steps.			
Walks, holding on to furniture.			
Picks up and puts down small toys.			
Stands alone.			
Sits down from standing.			

13-16 MONTHS

Bends or stoops and stands again.			
Puts small toys into a container.			
Hurls or throws objects.			
Walks well.			
Walks backward or sideways.			

17-20 MONTHS

	NO age ✓	ALMOST age ✓	YES age ✓
Walks while pushing, pulling, or carrying.	_____	_____	_____
Imitates simple motions.	_____	_____	_____
Climbs up and down furniture.	_____	_____	_____
Stands on one foot holding on.	_____	_____	_____
Walks, picks up a toy, and walks again.	_____	_____	_____

21-24 MONTHS

Jumps down from a low step.	_____	_____	_____
Kicks a ball.	_____	_____	_____
Runs forward.	_____	_____	_____
Stands up easily.	_____	_____	_____
Throws a ball overhand.	_____	_____	_____

25-30 MONTHS

Walks up and down stairs alone.	_____	_____	_____
Jumps in place two or more times.	_____	_____	_____
Runs or walks on tiptoe.	_____	_____	_____
Climbs on a jungle gym.	_____	_____	_____
Walks backward 10 or more feet.	_____	_____	_____

31-36 MONTHS

Jumps forward with feet together.	_____	_____	_____
Stands on one foot for 2 or more seconds.	_____	_____	_____
Steers and pedals a tricycle.	_____	_____	_____
Throws a ball underhand.	_____	_____	_____
Walks upstairs one foot on each step.	_____	_____	_____

37-42 MONTHS

	NO age ✓	ALMOST age ✓	YES age ✓
Walks downstairs one foot on each step.	____	____	____
Catches a large ball.	____	____	____
Runs around obstacles.	____	____	____
Hops in place on one foot.	____	____	____
Walks on a straight line or curb.	____	____	____

43-48 MONTHS

Hops forward on one foot two or more hops.	____	____	____
Catches a large bounced ball.	____	____	____
Gallops.	____	____	____
Walks forward heel touching toe.	____	____	____
Jumps over an object with both feet.	____	____	____

49-60 MONTHS

Catches a ball with hands.	____	____	____
Balances on tiptoes for 10 or more seconds.	____	____	____
Jumps over knee-high obstacles.	____	____	____
Walks backward toe touching heel.	____	____	____
Hops forward on one foot six or more hops.	____	____	____

61-72 MONTHS

Skips.	____	____	____
Touches toes without bending knees.	____	____	____
Rides a two-wheel bike.	____	____	____
Bounces and catches a ball with one hand.	____	____	____
Balances on one foot for 10 or more seconds.	____	____	____

2

The Checklist for Communicating

When you hear your child's first cries in the hospital, you are witnessing her announcement that she has arrived. As she develops, her cries begin to take on different meanings; she begins to laugh, coo, babble and then finally to speak.

Communicating evolves as your child learns to listen and understand others, while beginning to express herself. Listening and speaking are your child's attempts to communicate with others in her environment. During the early months, your child's communication is limited to crying, babbling, and otherwise vocalizing her needs and wants. These noises and your reactions to them helps your child develop comprehensible speech.

Your Child's Language Development

Children follow the same milestones and sequences in language development, regardless of physical differences. As they begin to interact with their environment, individual rates and styles of communicating will be unique.

Early language development is crucial. Lapses in language development from 2 to 6 years are not easy to make up. As the child's language gradually takes shape, it goes beyond simple listening and talking to being intertwined with thinking and mental development. Language is the single best predictor of scores on IQ tests and success in school. A parent can be concerned if, by 3 years, the child is not beginning to string words or is not understanding simple directions.

Toddlers have a great need to communicate. Language is how your child puts her world in order and plans her actions. Talking to herself and to others shows that she is thinking. Oral communication also is the groundwork for reading readiness.

How to Observe Your Child Communicating

Pay attention to your child's vocalizations—the babbles, the first words. Watch your child speak and listen attentively as she expresses herself. Monitor your child's hearing regularly (check her on the hearing items in the *Growing* section). Model (demonstrate) appropriate milestones, but otherwise allow language skills to occur naturally. Observe your child's interactions with others whenever possible, and note her interactions with you. Give your child plenty of time to initiate communication; it is just as important as encouraging her to respond to questions.

Completing the Communicating Section

Read through the *Communicating* items from beginning to end. Use the statements to help you visualize what to listen for, and refer to the Appendix for further explanation if needed. As you familiarize yourself with the *Communicating* behaviors, think about different situations where your child would naturally listen and speak. Prepare to provide those opportunities for your child to aid your observations and her development. Follow the guidelines in the Introduction for recording your observations.

Enriching Your Child's Language Development

Allow your child, from the time she is a very young infant, to listen and to express herself vocally. That means, respond to her babbles, coos, squeals, and other noises. From the first days home, talk to your new baby at every opportunity. Surround your child with language, with music, and with books. Explain and talk about everything you do to and with her. Get into the habit of describing and labeling the things you are doing with her and the things she touches, points to, and plays with. Provide opportunities and time for your child to communicate with those around her. Let her try new ways of talking and expressing herself without correcting her pronunciation and grammar. Converse with her to reinforce her communication. Create an environment rich with language in all its forms, and allow her to have many new language experiences and successes.

Read books to your baby, recite nursery rhymes, and sing to and with her. Give her the opportunity to converse with others—siblings, friends, and relatives. Let her talk to her toys and dolls in her play world. Audio recordings, children's videos, and TV programs, when used in moderation, can help to enrich a child's vocabulary. Use caution, however, since no experience is richer than real, natural, unpredictable communication with another person.

Communicating

0-4 MONTHS

	NO age ✓	ALMOST age ✓	YES age ✓
Coos and babbles.	_____	_____	_____
Makes a vowel sound.	_____	_____	_____
Laughs out loud.	_____	_____	_____
Responds to a voice.	_____	_____	_____
Makes sounds for attention.	_____	_____	_____

5-8 MONTHS

Makes three or more sounds in one breath.	_____	_____	_____
Says at least two different sounds like "da" and "ba."	_____	_____	_____
Makes sounds of at least two syllables.	_____	_____	_____
Responds to own name.	_____	_____	_____
Shouts.	_____	_____	_____

9-12 MONTHS

Imitates sounds.	_____	_____	_____
Listens to familiar words.	_____	_____	_____
Says "no" and shakes head.	_____	_____	_____
Says two or more words clearly to the parent.	_____	_____	_____
Uses Mama or Dada as names.	_____	_____	_____

13-16 MONTHS

Says four or more words clearly to others.	_____	_____	_____
Follows simple directions.	_____	_____	_____
Uses at least one word to express an idea.	_____	_____	_____
Asks for things by name.	_____	_____	_____
Makes up own meaningful words.	_____	_____	_____

17-20 MONTHS

	NO age ✓	ALMOST age ✓	YES age ✓
Listens to music or stories for 3 or more minutes.	____	____	____
Uses 10 or more words.	____	____	____
Babbles or talks into a play phone.	____	____	____
Answers simple questions.	____	____	____
Names most familiar objects.	____	____	____

21-24 MONTHS

Uses 20 or more words.	____	____	____
Answers "What is your name?"	____	____	____
Imitates new words.	____	____	____
Repeats at least one line of a rhyme or song.	____	____	____
Uses at least two words together.	____	____	____

25-30 MONTHS

Imitates parent's tone of voice.	____	____	____
Repeats parts of songs and rhymes.	____	____	____
Uses sentences of at least three words.	____	____	____
Uses personal pronouns *I, you, me.*	____	____	____
Asks questions.	____	____	____

31-36 MONTHS

Takes part in a conversation.	____	____	____
Answers "who, where, and when" questions.	____	____	____
Adds many new words each month.	____	____	____
Tells what to do when hungry, thirsty, sleepy, etc.	____	____	____
Uses *in, on, empty,* and *full.*	____	____	____

37-42 MONTHS

	NO age ✓	ALMOST age ✓	YES age ✓
Talks clearly.	_____	_____	_____
Tells what is happening in pictures.	_____	_____	_____
Uses plurals.	_____	_____	_____
Uses *the* and *a*.	_____	_____	_____
Knows all the words to a song or rhyme.	_____	_____	_____

43-48 MONTHS

Talks about imaginary situations.	_____	_____	_____
Listens to stories for 20 minutes or longer.	_____	_____	_____
Plays with words; makes up new words.	_____	_____	_____
Uses four or five words for feelings.	_____	_____	_____
Laughs at and uses silly rhyming.	_____	_____	_____

49-60 MONTHS

Clearly says own first and last names.	_____	_____	_____
Can argue with words.	_____	_____	_____
Uses jokes and silly language.	_____	_____	_____
Uses sentences of at least five words.	_____	_____	_____
Makes "b, p, m, w, h, d, t, n, g, k, ng, y" sounds.	_____	_____	_____

61-72 MONTHS

Gives full name, age, and address.	_____	_____	_____
Talks about own feelings.	_____	_____	_____
Identifies the first sound in words.	_____	_____	_____
Uses well-constructed sentences.	_____	_____	_____
Shares experiences with others.	_____	_____	_____

3

The Checklist for Relating

Your child's first meaningful relationship is that impenetrable bond with you. From that first human connection, your child begins to relate with her siblings, relatives, and other children. These relationships unfold first at home, and then during play with other children. Nothing is more heart-warming than when you hear the sound of children's laughter in play—a signal that your child is truly learning to relate positively to others.

Relating includes the social and emotional milestones encountered in establishing relationships with others. The relationships your child develops with others in the first months and years shape her social skills later in life. During infancy, your child's relationships are measured by her reactions to others—by smiling, vocalizing, and preferring to be in the company of others. As she grows, play becomes the avenue to develop her social relationships.

The values and attitudes of your family shape your child's social behaviors. How conflicts are handled, affection is demonstrated, and moods are expressed in the home are important to your child's social development. Your discipline, affection, and opinion of your child shape her self-concept, which will be carried with her through life.

Your Child's Social Development

Children follow the same milestones and sequences in social development, regardless of personality differences. As they learn to relate to others, their individual rates and styles of relating are unique to each child's personality.

Play is your child's work; it provides her the chance to learn how to relate to others. Through play and the development of relationships, your young child's personality begins to emerge. Fantasy and make-believe are important aspects in your child's play, as long as they do not exclude interactions with others. Make-believe gives your child the opportunity to act out different roles, practice handling situations, and exercise her imagination.

Desirable qualities like sharing and self-confidence develop through your child's experiences with others. As she experiences conflicts, she learns how to work things out—first within the smaller family group, then later in larger groups. Rules are important from the beginning; they develop into codes of behavior for your child. It is never too early for the parent to establish a few rules, and then stick to them.

How to Observe Your Child's Social Development

Give your child many different opportunities to play and interact with others. Watch your child as she begins to relate to you, her toys, her siblings, and then to other children and adults. If your child is the only child at home, it is a good idea to allow her to be part of a play group or spend play time with other children so that you may observe her interactions.

Completing the Relating Section

Read through the *Relating* items from beginning to end. Use the statements to help you visualize what you will be looking for, and refer to the Appendix for further explanation if needed. As you familiarize yourself with the *Relating* behaviors, think about different situations where your child would naturally show those behaviors. Prepare to provide those opportunities for your child to aid your observations and her development. Follow the guidelines in the Introduction for recording your observations.

Enriching Your Child's Social Development

The "climate" in the home sets the stage for your child's positive relationships with others. Your home environment must be responsive for your child to flourish. Parents should be united, consistent in discipline, and tolerant of phases in social and emotional growth. You can help foster positive relationships and personality-building by being loving, relaxed, responsive, and understanding. Resist interfering or intervening in your child's interactions.

Though it is tough to let go and allow your child to depend on herself in conflict situations, it is very important that you do.

Watch other children in group play; it may help ease your concerns about your own child. Encourage happiness. Exhibit the behavior you desire from your child; model how she should interact with others. When disciplining your child, be consistent, reasonable, and allow her to experience the natural consequences of her behavior.

Make your child feel needed by welcoming her help when she offers it. Allow time and opportunity for your child to be by herself when she wants it—balance social time with alone time. Encourage her to recognize and express her emotions and moods.

Relating

0-4 MONTHS

	NO age ✓	ALMOST age ✓	YES age ✓
Shows excitement.	_____	_____	_____
Makes sounds or moves to get attention.	_____	_____	_____
Shows interest in mirror image.	_____	_____	_____
Plays with own hands.	_____	_____	_____
Smiles and laughs when talked to.	_____	_____	_____

5-8 MONTHS

Smiles and laughs at baby games.	_____	_____	_____
Wants parents and siblings over strangers.	_____	_____	_____
Cries when separated from parent.	_____	_____	_____
Touches or smiles at mirror image.	_____	_____	_____
Shows pleasure and displeasure.	_____	_____	_____

9-12 MONTHS

Shows moods by looking hurt, happy, or sad.	_____	_____	_____
Plays with adults or older children.	_____	_____	_____
Plays pat-a-cake, peek-a-boo, and so-big.	_____	_____	_____
Offers toys to others.	_____	_____	_____
Seeks approval and responds to "no."	_____	_____	_____

13-16 MONTHS

Smiles easily and shows affection for others.	_____	_____	_____
Gives a toy without wanting it back immediately.	_____	_____	_____
Enjoys being around children.	_____	_____	_____
Plays chase me/catch me games.	_____	_____	_____
Expresses many emotions.	_____	_____	_____

17-20 MONTHS

	NO age ✓	ALMOST age ✓	YES age ✓
Demands the company of others.	_____	_____	_____
Enjoys rough-house play with parent.	_____	_____	_____
Spends time looking at self in mirror.	_____	_____	_____
Helps others.	_____	_____	_____
Shows off.	_____	_____	_____

21-24 MONTHS

Talks to self or to toys when playing.	_____	_____	_____
Plays alone in the company of other children.	_____	_____	_____
Shares attention.	_____	_____	_____
Likes to please others.	_____	_____	_____
Orders others around.	_____	_____	_____

25-30 MONTHS

Imitates mannerisms of parent.	_____	_____	_____
Shows affection for a friend.	_____	_____	_____
Tests parent's reaction to "no."	_____	_____	_____
Relates feelings with gestures and words.	_____	_____	_____
Calls others "Baby," "Mommy," and "Daddy."	_____	_____	_____

31-36 MONTHS

Plays cooperatively with another child.	_____	_____	_____
Pretends.	_____	_____	_____
Shows disgust.	_____	_____	_____
Shows interest in TV.	_____	_____	_____
Plays in a group.	_____	_____	_____

37-42 MONTHS

	NO age ✓	ALMOST age ✓	YES age ✓
Calls attention to own performance.	_____	_____	_____
Interacts with other children.	_____	_____	_____
Shows sympathy toward others.	_____	_____	_____
Spends extended time in favorite activities.	_____	_____	_____
Is friendly and agreeable.	_____	_____	_____

43-48 MONTHS

Shares toys.	_____	_____	_____
Shows self-control.	_____	_____	_____
Takes part in group activities.	_____	_____	_____
Is attached to one friend.	_____	_____	_____
Respects others and their things.	_____	_____	_____

49-60 MONTHS

Prefers same-sex friends.	_____	_____	_____
Enjoys performing for others.	_____	_____	_____
Whispers and has secrets.	_____	_____	_____
Responds to praise and blame.	_____	_____	_____
Prefers other children over adults.	_____	_____	_____

61-72 MONTHS

Shows socially acceptable behavior.	_____	_____	_____
Follows classroom rules and directions.	_____	_____	_____
Participates in competitive play.	_____	_____	_____
Initiates social contacts.	_____	_____	_____
Accepts fair play and fair punishment.	_____	_____	_____

4

The Checklist for Thinking

It is no wonder that every parent sees their child as a genius, when we watch in amazement as she reveals her own independent thoughts. As she grows, she learns at an incredible pace. *Thinking* involves those observable behaviors that reflect your child's growing intellect and ability to think and solve problems. Before too long, your child will be going to school. Thinking skills are critical to school success and school success greatly influences self-esteem. Love of thinking and learning are necessary for creative thinking in her future.

Exploration is the basis for thinking. Exploration as it occurs in moving, communicating, relating, and in other aspects of development provides opportunity for problem solving and creative thinking.

Your Child's Intellectual Development

Children follow the same milestones and sequences in intellectual development, regardless of individual differences. As they explore their environment and solve problems, their thinking abilities and memory capabilities emerge uniquely according to each child's own individual rate and style of development.

Your child uses her senses to explore, learn, and practice with objects in her own world. She develops the ability to deal with symbols like letters and numbers necessary for skill building in school. It's necessary that your child pass though certain thinking stages in order to take the next step. No matter how much we try to teach, children must experience the sequences of thought development when they are ready. Intellectual development should not be pushed, but rather, the child must be exposed to a stimulating environment that invites exploration and learning.

How to Observe Your Child's Thinking Skills

Provide activities where you can watch your child play and manipulate objects that involve all of the senses. Don't direct your child to solve something. Instead, present an activity and watch long enough to see if problem solving occurs naturally. If she is eager to talk while she is thinking, listen to her comments—they will reveal much about what she is thinking.

Your child should want to try, to explore, to build, and to scribble. These activities should not be forced or given as a test. Overall interest in thinking is as important to intellectual development as the ability to solve a problem.

Completing the Thinking Section

Read through the *Thinking* items from beginning to end. Use the statements to help you visualize what you will be looking for, and refer to the Appendix for further explanation if needed. As you familiarize yourself with the *Thinking* behaviors, consider different situations where your child would naturally show those behaviors. Prepare to provide those opportunities for your child to aid your observations and her development. Follow the guidelines in the Introduction for recording your observations.

Enriching Your Child's Intellectual Development

The environment you create at home is the best single predictor of school achievement. It has proven to be the greatest influence on your child's general ability to learn. When you answer and ask questions, you create an environment that satisfies your child's curiosity and improves her self-esteem.

Praise your child as she tries to solve new problems. Comment and make little suggestions that will lead to successes—for example, "Try it this way," or "I wonder what would happen if you . . ." Resist directing, fixing, or adjusting your child's work. Encourage your child to do what she likes doing and build upon that. Introduce and have available a variety of toys—like puzzles, books, blocks, and containers. Provide activities that use all of the senses—sight, sound, taste, touch, and smell. If it's part of your child's exploration and creative process, go ahead and let her make a mess. Be tolerant when your child repeats something incessantly. Often, children must experiment or repeat something many times to learn one idea, like turning a light switch on and off, or repeating a question over and over again.

Encourage curiosity and creativity. Promote your child's self-confidence by letting her tackle new experiences. You can facilitate lifelong learning by supporting and encouraging your child's exploration.

Thinking

0-4 MONTHS

	NO age ✓	ALMOST age ✓	YES age ✓
Follows moving toy with eyes.	___	___	___
Mouths nearly everything.	___	___	___
Turns head and looks toward a sound.	___	___	___
Touches the facial features of others.	___	___	___
Recognizes family members.	___	___	___

5-8 MONTHS

Watches a toy being hidden and then looks for it.	___	___	___
Pulls a string in order to get a toy.	___	___	___
Holds a toy and reaches for another.	___	___	___
Explores own body with mouth and hands.	___	___	___
Explores by touching, shaking, and tasting objects.	___	___	___

9-12 MONTHS

Holds three small toys at the same time.	___	___	___
Finds a hidden toy.	___	___	___
Uses an object as a container for another.	___	___	___
Imitates actions like scribbling or bell ringing.	___	___	___
Holds a toy and explores with the other hand.	___	___	___

13-16 MONTHS

Fits a round piece into a simple puzzle.	___	___	___
Turns toys right side up.	___	___	___
Puts a small object in a bottle and dumps it out.	___	___	___
Scribbles with a pencil or crayon.	___	___	___
Points to one or more named body parts.	___	___	___

17-20 MONTHS

	NO age ✓	ALMOST age ✓	YES age ✓
Knows what to do with a hammer, a phone, etc.	_____	_____	_____
Imitates housework.	_____	_____	_____
Points to four or more named body parts.	_____	_____	_____
Puts together a simple two-piece puzzle.	_____	_____	_____
Uses chairs to reach things.	_____	_____	_____

21-24 MONTHS

Makes a circle, a line, or a "V" after watching.	_____	_____	_____
Looks for ways to work new toys.	_____	_____	_____
Names four or more pictures.	_____	_____	_____
Nests boxes, cups, and stacking rings.	_____	_____	_____
Puts together a simple three-piece puzzle.	_____	_____	_____

25-30 MONTHS

Waits when told "in a minute," "later," or "pretty soon."	_____	_____	_____
Understands consequences of actions.	_____	_____	_____
Builds a six-block tower.	_____	_____	_____
Confines scribbles to the page.	_____	_____	_____
Brings *one* of something.	_____	_____	_____

31-36 MONTHS

Strings three large beads.	_____	_____	_____
Draws a person (shows head and legs).	_____	_____	_____
Builds with blocks.	_____	_____	_____
Understands *in, out, in front of, under, over,* etc.	_____	_____	_____
Turns pages of a book one-by-one.	_____	_____	_____

37-42 MONTHS

	NO age ✓	ALMOST age ✓	YES age ✓
Differentiates a boy from a girl.	_____	_____	_____
Counts to 10.	_____	_____	_____
Identifies two or more familiar objects by touch.	_____	_____	_____
Talks about pictures seen in books.	_____	_____	_____
Follows two-step directions.	_____	_____	_____

43-48 MONTHS

Matches pictures in simple memory games.	_____	_____	_____
Points to triangle, circle, rectangle, and square.	_____	_____	_____
Remembers recent events.	_____	_____	_____
Draws a person (head, legs, arms, trunk, shoulders).	_____	_____	_____
Copies a circle.	_____	_____	_____

49-60 MONTHS

Cuts following a line.	_____	_____	_____
Knows simple opposites.	_____	_____	_____
Knows about the seasons and related activities.	_____	_____	_____
Names at least four colors.	_____	_____	_____
Counts three objects by pointing.	_____	_____	_____

61-72 MONTHS

Copies capital letters (O, V, H, and T).	_____	_____	_____
Counts three to five fingers and tells how many.	_____	_____	_____
Matches a printed number with objects.	_____	_____	_____
Sorts objects by size, color, and shape.	_____	_____	_____
Points to named numbers.	_____	_____	_____

5

The Checklist for Adapting

In the beginning, you are awestruck at the total, complete, and utter dependence of this tiny little being on you. While at times you may feel overwhelmed, this dependency is actually the beginning of her 18-year odyssey toward independence.

Adapting includes all those basic skills—like eating, dressing, and toileting—needed for your child to become independent. These adapting behaviors are necessary to build your child's confidence, good health, and self-help skills. Your child's self-concept is closely related to how well she can do things for herself. When your child is able take care of her own basic personal needs, she will be less dependent on you and better prepared to attend school.

How Your Child's Independence Develops

Children follow the same milestones and sequences in adaptive development, regardless of individual differences. As they learn to accomplish basic routine tasks on their own, independence is expressed uniquely according to each child's own individual rate and style of development.

Your child's earliest signs of adaptation will appear as her eating and sleeping schedules fall into a regular routine, and then become less frequent. Most parents anxiously look forward to a major adapting milestone—sleeping through the night. As she develops, your child will begin to feed herself, to play on her own, and then be ready for toilet learning. She will soon be able to dress and groom herself, and before you know it, she will be ready to go to school.

How to Observe Your Child's Independence

Watch your child during her daily routines. Allow many opportunities for her to do things for herself, even if it takes longer or makes a mess. Watch her as she tries to accomplish the task by herself. Don't force the situation; if she doesn't want to do it, wait until she is ready.

Completing the Adapting Section

Read through the *Adapting* items from beginning to end. Use the statements to help you visualize what you will be looking for, and refer to the Appendix for further explanation if needed. As you familiarize yourself with the *Adapting* behaviors, think about different situations where your child would naturally show those behaviors. Prepare to provide those opportunities for your child to aid your observations and her development. Follow the guidelines in the Introduction for recording your observations.

Enriching Your Child's Independence

Praise your child and make little suggestions that will lead to successes—for example, "You try to do this." Establish eating, toileting, and dressing routines very early. Regular schedules encourage acceptance of good routines and habits. During finicky eating periods, have good foods on hand. Ages 2, 3, and 4 are the best years for developing food tastes. The amounts your child eats and wants will vary from meal to meal, day to day, week to week, and month to month. Offer small portions and encourage your child to ask for more. Meals should be social and a time to try new foods and use table manners. It's best not to introduce conflict by requiring her to eat certain foods or amounts of foods.

When developing independence in toileting, don't discipline your child or make it a struggle. Read through the behaviors for toileting and note the average ages when these behaviors are usually established. Toilet learning should not be pushed when your child is not ready.

At a very young age, your child can help with dressing. As she gets older, let her try to manipulate buttons, zippers, and more complicated clothing. Resist directing, fixing, or adjusting her attempts at dressing. Praise your child when she tries to dress herself. Hang clothes on a low clothes rack or put them in a reachable drawer in a dresser, so that your toddler can begin to choose her own clothes. Part of dressing is putting clothes away and in the laundry—encourage your child to accomplish these chores too.

When she is a young toddler, your child will want to help you with simple chores around the house. These behaviors should be encouraged and praised. As she approaches school age, she should be assigned simple chores as her complete responsibility on a regular basis. Encourage your child to play with or be with other children to help develop her independence away from you. Leave her with a relative or baby-sitter once in a while to help her learn to function without you.

Adapting

0-4 MONTHS

	NO age ✓	ALMOST age ✓	YES age ✓
Eats regularly and waits to be fed.	_____	_____	_____
Gets excited at feeding preparations.	_____	_____	_____
Shows awareness of strangers.	_____	_____	_____
Feeds no more than once during the night.	_____	_____	_____
Responds to parent's presence.	_____	_____	_____

5-8 MONTHS

Eats baby food.	_____	_____	_____
Feeds self finger foods.	_____	_____	_____
Holds own bottle to drink.	_____	_____	_____
Refuses things.	_____	_____	_____
Shows attachment to parent.	_____	_____	_____

9-12 MONTHS

Holds cup to drink.	_____	_____	_____
Occupies self for 10 minutes or longer.	_____	_____	_____
Cooperates during dressing.	_____	_____	_____
Holds a spoon at meal time.	_____	_____	_____
Chooses toys deliberately.	_____	_____	_____

13-16 MONTHS

Brings things to an adult for fixing or for help.	_____	_____	_____
Seats self in a chair for short periods of time.	_____	_____	_____
Discards the bottle.	_____	_____	_____
Indicates wet or soiled diaper.	_____	_____	_____
Makes wants known.	_____	_____	_____

17-20 MONTHS

	NO age ✓	ALMOST age ✓	YES age ✓
Eats without help.	_____	_____	_____
Leads adults to things.	_____	_____	_____
Helps with dressing.	_____	_____	_____
Puts on shoes.	_____	_____	_____
Zips and unzips.	_____	_____	_____

21-24 MONTHS

	NO	ALMOST	YES
Asks for food or drink.	_____	_____	_____
Puts toys away with encouragement.	_____	_____	_____
Eats table food including cut meats.	_____	_____	_____
Shares attention.	_____	_____	_____
Turns knobs and opens doors.	_____	_____	_____

25-30 MONTHS

	NO	ALMOST	YES
Puts on simple clothing.	_____	_____	_____
Cooperates in washing hands.	_____	_____	_____
Asks to use the toilet.	_____	_____	_____
Cooperates in brushing teeth.	_____	_____	_____
Follows routines at meals, bedtime, etc.	_____	_____	_____

31-36 MONTHS

	NO	ALMOST	YES
Initiates purposeful, often brief conversations.	_____	_____	_____
Is orderly.	_____	_____	_____
Avoids danger.	_____	_____	_____
Takes turns.	_____	_____	_____
Shows clothing preferences.	_____	_____	_____

37-42 MONTHS

	NO age ✓	ALMOST age ✓	YES age ✓
Puts on own shoes, pants, and underwear.	_____	_____	_____
Undresses.	_____	_____	_____
Feeds self neatly.	_____	_____	_____
Separates from parent with little fuss.	_____	_____	_____
Focuses on a task without being distracted.	_____	_____	_____

43-48 MONTHS

Puts shoes on correct feet.	_____	_____	_____
Uses a fork and a spoon.	_____	_____	_____
Uses the toilet without help.	_____	_____	_____
Does one or more household chores.	_____	_____	_____
Helps with easy meals.	_____	_____	_____

49-60 MONTHS

Washes own hands and face.	_____	_____	_____
Completely dresses self.	_____	_____	_____
Asks for bathroom privacy.	_____	_____	_____
Pours liquid into a glass.	_____	_____	_____
Starts and finishes easy projects.	_____	_____	_____

61-72 MONTHS

Goes to bed when told.	_____	_____	_____
Crosses the street safely.	_____	_____	_____
Laces and ties shoes.	_____	_____	_____
Bathes or showers alone.	_____	_____	_____
Brushes own teeth thoroughly.	_____	_____	_____

6

The Checklist for Growing

Every time you turn around, your child has outgrown yet another pair of shoes. This is just one symbol of the phenomenal growth that occurs from birth to 6.

Growing involves the facets of physical development usually monitored by your child's health care providers, like nurses, doctors, and dentists. Growth gains in height, weight, head circumference, and reflexes are the primary ways your pediatrician learns if your child is developing normally. Other important growth milestones are immunizations and the emergence of teeth.

Without adequate sleep, your child's body cannot grow optimally. Everyone's body needs rest to repair and build from the day's activities. Adequate sleep is necessary for efficient thinking, moving, and relating, and is crucial to growing.

How Your Child Grows

Children follow the same milestones in physical growth, but vary in their individual rates. You can expect proportional weight and height or length gains; a child should be getting taller or longer as she gains weight. As your child develops, she will require less total sleep, and be able to sleep for longer periods. Vaccinations, immunizations, and hearing and vision screenings are important during the early years to ensure your child's healthy growth.

How to Observe Your Child's Physical Growth

Schedule checkups with your pediatrician to have your child weighed and measured at regular intervals. Track sleep patterns for 1 week and compute the average sleep time. Keep track of your child's teething by counting her teeth. Look at your child's posture and walking pattern. Watch your child when she is around other children of the same age to become aware of general physical development at your child's age, but realize that there are individual differences.

Completing the Growing Section

Read through the *Growing* items from beginning to end. Use the statements to help you visualize what you will be looking for, and refer to the Appendix for further explanation if needed. As you familiarize yourself with the *Growing* behaviors, think about different situations where your child would naturally be evaluated (at a physical exam, a dental exam, or school screenings). Follow the guidelines in the Introduction for recording your child's growth.

Enriching Your Child's Physical Growth

Encourage your child to eat a variety of healthy foods by having them available. Don't offer rewards or force your child to eat things she doesn't want to eat. Praise her for trying, smelling, tasting, and touching new foods. Consult your pediatrician for tips about how your child's diet might be improved to reduce fats and sugars and increase foods low in fats and sugars.

Don't become overanxious to teach your child to use the toilet. Treat it as any other activity — make it fun by allowing the child to choose when she would like to try. Encourage and present opportunities to try any parts of the activity. Don't let toileting or a lack of interest on your child's part control you. When you have evidence that a child can pull her pants up and down, control sphincters, flush the toilet, notice wet or soiled diapers, and realize that she is about to urinate or have a bowel movement, then seriously encourage toileting.

Encourage routines and allow rituals. Schedule regular exams according to your pediatrician's recommendations. Bring *Test Your Child: Birth to 6* to your child's physical exams. Choose a pediatric dentist and schedule regular checkups. Most recommend the first visit when your child has all 20 baby teeth (at about 36 months).

Encourage good habits — dental care, physical exams, hand-washing, not sharing personal hygienic tools (toothbrushes, combs, hair brushes, etc.), eating regularly, eating a variety of foods, and sleeping and resting appropriately. Recognize when your child is tired and encourage rest or a quiet activity. Every day encourage your child to participate in engaging play, interacting with others, large muscle movements, and exploration — activities that will naturally result in hunger, thirst, and the need for rest.

Growing

0-4 MONTHS

	NO age ✓	ALMOST age ✓	YES age ✓
Weighs 10 to 18 pounds.	_____	_____	_____
Measures 23 to 27 inches.	_____	_____	_____
Hears well — responds to a voice in a quiet setting.	_____	_____	_____
Has two of three DTP* and polio vaccinations.	_____	_____	_____
Sleeps a total of 11 to 18 hours.	_____	_____	_____

5-8 MONTHS

Weighs 14 to 23 pounds.	_____	_____	_____
Measures 25 to 30 inches.	_____	_____	_____
Has third and final DTP vaccination.	_____	_____	_____
Has two to four teeth.	_____	_____	_____
Sleeps a total of 9 to 18 hours.	_____	_____	_____

9-12 MONTHS

Weighs 17 to 27 pounds.	_____	_____	_____
Measures 27 to 32 inches.	_____	_____	_____
Has five to seven teeth.	_____	_____	_____
Has tuberculin and hematocrit or hemoglobin tests.	_____	_____	_____
Hears well — responds to a voice in a quiet setting.	_____	_____	_____

13-16 MONTHS

Weighs 17 to 29 pounds.	_____	_____	_____
Measures 27 to 33 inches.	_____	_____	_____
Has eight to ten teeth.	_____	_____	_____
Has measles, mumps, and rubella vaccinations.	_____	_____	_____
Sleeps a total of 9 to 12 hours.	_____	_____	_____

*Abbreviation denoting the vaccination against diphtheria, tetanus, and pertussis (whooping cough).

17-20 MONTHS

	NO age ✓	ALMOST age ✓	YES age ✓
Weighs 18 to 32 pounds.	_____	_____	_____
Measures 29 to 36 inches.	_____	_____	_____
Has 11 to 15 teeth.	_____	_____	_____
Has DTP booster and final polio vaccination.	_____	_____	_____
Hears well — responds to a voice in a quiet setting.	_____	_____	_____

21-24 MONTHS

	NO	ALMOST	YES
Weighs 21 to 33 pounds.	_____	_____	_____
Measures 31 to 37 inches.	_____	_____	_____
Has 16 to 18 teeth.	_____	_____	_____
Has influenza (Hib*) immunization.	_____	_____	_____
Sleeps a total of 9 to 12 hours.	_____	_____	_____

25-30 MONTHS

	NO	ALMOST	YES
Weighs 22 to 35 pounds.	_____	_____	_____
Measures 32 to 39 inches.	_____	_____	_____
Has a dry diaper after napping.	_____	_____	_____
Has 18 to 20 teeth.	_____	_____	_____
Hears well — responds to directions.	_____	_____	_____

31-36 MONTHS

	NO	ALMOST	YES
Weighs 24 to 38 pounds.	_____	_____	_____
Measures 34 to 41 inches.	_____	_____	_____
Has 20 teeth.	_____	_____	_____
Sleeps a total of 9 to 12 hours.	_____	_____	_____
Has dental examination.	_____	_____	_____

*Abbreviation for the bacterium *Haemophilus influenzae* type B.

37-42 MONTHS

	NO age ✓	ALMOST age ✓	YES age ✓
Weighs 25 to 40 pounds.	_____	_____	_____
Measures 35 to 42 inches.	_____	_____	_____
Legs lengthen and stomach flattens.	_____	_____	_____
Hears well — responds to a whisper.	_____	_____	_____
Sees well.	_____	_____	_____

43-48 MONTHS

Weighs 27 to 43 pounds.	_____	_____	_____
Measures 36 to 44 inches.	_____	_____	_____
Naps briefly or not at all.	_____	_____	_____
Sleeps a total of 9 to 12 hours.	_____	_____	_____
Has the proportions of a child rather than a toddler.	_____	_____	_____

49-60 MONTHS

Weighs 30 to 50 pounds.	_____	_____	_____
Measures 38 to 46 inches.	_____	_____	_____
Has had DTP and polio booster shots.	_____	_____	_____
Passes hearing screening.	_____	_____	_____
Responds to standard "E" chart eye test.	_____	_____	_____

61-72 MONTHS

Weighs 33 to 57 pounds.	_____	_____	_____
Measures 42 to 49 inches.	_____	_____	_____
Feet have arches and legs are straight.	_____	_____	_____
Has fewer colds and flu.	_____	_____	_____
Passes scoliosis/posture screening.	_____	_____	_____

PART 2

Activities

7

Activities to Enhance Moving

It is often said that children develop in spite of our well-intentioned teaching. Often, all we really need to do is to provide ample chances for our children to explore on their own. Below is a laundry list of movement-based activities to introduce to your son or daughter. Consider the list a springboard from which you can launch into your own ideas for enhancing your child's development. Take the ideas listed below and make them work for you, for your child, and for your family. While some ideas may seem simplistic and repetitive, they are perfect for most children. If your child wants to do the same thing over and over, that is perfectly normal and should be encouraged. If your child turns away, struggles, resists, or otherwise indicates she doesn't want to participate, listen to her. Children are notorious for disliking something once, then adoring it the next time, so don't give up—try, try again.

Play is "child's work," and your baby should spend much of her waking alert times in some sort of play. While the play activities listed below are organized into developmental categories, it is important to remember that play in one area develops all areas.

It is important to allow and encourage your child to explore her environment with as much independence and self-motivation as is safe for her age. As your child grows, her need for your supervision, direction, and motivation will vary. You might come to realize that your child resists your attempts to "teach" her. Listen to her. Allow her to explore and learn on her own. Provide the materials and the opportunities your baby likes and you will enrich all development. Don't become frustrated if your child doesn't "perform." Remember, it is the process, not the outcome, that will create that special bond only you and your baby can have.

When your newborn has come home from the hospital, family members together should walk through the house or apartment to "child-proof" the environment for safety. It won't be long before the tiny baby will be moving around on her own. Remove all small objects from low shelves, place safety catches on cabinets, plug all empty electrical outlets, remove loose electrical, curtain, and mini-blind cords and cat litter boxes, and keep the floor clean. While independence is important, your child should never be completely unsupervised or allowed to use toys, tools, or appliances not intended for children her chronological or developmental age.

The most important principle in enhancing motor development is experience. You must let your baby move, crawl, and physically explore her environment. Parents who carry their babies on their hips much of the time are impeding their children's growth and development. From the earliest stages in infancy, place your child on a flat blanket (not a comforter) on the floor or in a "playpen." Let her move, wiggle, roll, stretch, and reach. As she becomes a toddler, she will wear you out with her constant movements and short attention span. Your role is to provide a safe, supervised environment for her to explore, and then let her go! Infants and toddlers who are allowed to be physically active enter school with good coordination, strength, and stamina.

Before expecting a particular "performance," let your child explore the objects, toys, and environment she is in. When she seems comfortable, encourage her to try an activity. The activities below link directly to the items in the checklist. If your child has scored "low" on a particular motor behavior that you think she should be able to do, study the activity in the list below and incorporate it into your child's routine. Feel free to adapt or expand the activity to suit your home and situation. Most of all, have fun with these activities! Although they are designed to practice and reinforce specific movements, they can not be successful until they're brought to life; only you can make the learning process fun.

0-4 Months

Head Up

Hold your baby seated on your lap facing you. Support her by holding her under her arms and around her chest and back. Talk to her in a pleasing voice in this position for about 10 seconds, and watch to see how steady she holds her head up.

Decorate your baby's crib and play area, at baby eye level, with photographs of other babies, to stimulate her to hold her head up as she is looking around. Hang mobiles, posters, and toys over your baby's crib, changing area, and play areas. Lie on your back and view them to be sure they are fun and interesting for your baby to look at.

Toy Grab

While your baby is alert, lying on her back or seated in an infant seat, hold an enticing, brightly colored rattle or other infant toy in front of her chest within her reach. Shake, rattle, and move the toy around. Capture her attention and encourage her to reach for and grab the rattle.

Place rattles and other safe toys in your baby's hand. Move her hand for her so that the rattle makes noise and so that she can see it. Place all kinds of safe toys all around well within your baby's reach.

Rolling

While your baby is awake and content, place her on her side on a flat blanket on the floor. Sit facing her back and talk to her to encourage her to roll over to see you. Use a rattle, musical toy, or other pleasant sound to capture her attention. Roll your baby gently from side to side so that she can experience the feeling of rolling as well as to see the world from all different angles.

Sitting

Seat your baby supported by pillows. Face her and talk to her, give her a rattle, and engage her attention for about 10 seconds. Watch to see if she is able to stay sitting without slumping. If she slumps over, prop her up again and do not leave her in this position unsupervised.

Hold your baby in a sitting position from different angles—from in front of her, from her side, and behind her.

Decorate the part of the car seat your baby sees when traveling in the car. If she spends a lot of time in her car seat, change the decorations.

Seat your baby in an infant seat, carefully strapped in, and play with her.

Pull your baby up to sitting gently and carefully by her arms.

Put your baby in a sitting position, placing her hands on the floor between her legs so that her arms are supporting her weight.

The Seal

Place your baby on her stomach on a flat blanket on the floor. Sit in front of her 3 to 5 feet away. Capture her attention by clapping your hands, talking to her, or shaking a rattle near your face. Watch to see if she pushes up, straightens her arms, and lifts her head up to look at you.

5-8 Months

Creeping and Crawling

Place your baby on her tummy on the floor in an unobstructed, clean area. Sit 5 or more feet away from her and attract her attention with your voice or a rattle, then encourage her to come to you. Lie on the floor near her and talk to her, saying things like "Come to me so I can kiss you" or "I love you" or "You are so sweet, I'm gonna eat you for dessert." You may move closer if she is only able to move a very short distance, or farther away if she easily comes to you. Reward her with your voice, your touch, or by giving her the rattle or toy as soon as she reaches you.

Help your baby move forward by letting her push against you with her feet while she lies on the floor. Praise her efforts by moving a toy a little closer, tickling her, and telling her how strong she is.

Passing the Toy

Place a toy in your baby's hand when she is sitting up or in an infant seat. Do not distract her, but let her focus on the toy. Watch to see if she passes the toy to her other hand, and even back again without dropping it. If she drops the toy, give it back to her as long as her attention allows.

Put toys in your baby's hands. Provide toys that she can easily hold, like soft balls with grips, rattles, brightly colored light objects, and soft fabric books.

Standing Up

Hold your baby up under her arms with your hands around her back and chest. Let her support her weight with her legs and bend and straighten her knees, so she bounces up and down as she likes. Sing songs to her and tell her what she is doing.

Seat your baby on the floor in front of you. Let her grasp onto both of your hands or fingers, and then pull gradually, encouraging her to use her feet and legs to pull up to a standing position. Do it again, only let her do all the pulling, to see if she can pull herself up, and encourage her by making it fun, and making comments like, "Let's stand up!" "Whee!" or "What a big girl!"

Stand your baby up against upholstered furniture, supporting and protecting her from falls. Help her shift her weight from one foot to the other by gently rocking her from one side to the other. This is a good time to sing little songs or repeat little rhymes like "Pony Boy," and so forth.

Place your baby near a low padded couch, chair, or sturdy stool, and put a favored toy on the furniture within your baby's range of vision. Shake the toy and talk to your baby, saying things like "Come get the toy," or "What is your toy doing up here—can you get it back?" Praise and reward her efforts by giv-ing her the toy or standing her up to get it.

Pincer Pickup

During mealtime, place small pieces of your baby's food in front of her. Make sure she watches as you pick up a piece, put it in her fingers, and then to her mouth so she can eat it. Watch then to see if she picks up a morsel on her own, using her thumb and forefinger, rather than her whole hand.

Walking Motion

Seat your baby on the floor in front of you. While on your knees, face her, grasp her hands, and gradually pull her to a standing position. Then "walk" back-ward on your knees, encouraging your baby to walk forward a few steps. Talk to her while she is walking and make it a fun activity.

Hold your baby by her hands in a standing position and let her support her own weight as you stand behind and above her. When she can do this confi-dently, shift her weight from side to side by gently rocking her while you walk forward with your legs on either side of her.

9-12 Months

Creeping Up the Stairs

Sit on the floor with your baby facing toward several upward steps. Place a toy on the third step where she can see it. Point to it so she notices it. Then tell her to go up the stairs. If needed, help her crawl forward, placing her hands on the first step. As she moves upward, stay directly behind or over her for safety.

Cruising

Place your baby in a standing position holding on at one end of a sofa. Place a toy at the other end of the sofa. Encourage her to "walk," holding on to the sofa with one or both hands, to get to the toy. If she sits down, raise her back to standing, and encourage her to continue, praising her as she moves along.

Stand your baby up along a couch or longer low table. Sit opposite your baby and call to her while holding out your hands.

Toy Pickup

Sit down on the floor with your baby. Find several safe toys the size of your baby's palm. Place the toys on the floor within her reach, and encourage her to pick each one of them up. Make it fun by saying something like "Where's the kitty?" Then point to it, and watch to see if she picks it up. Be sure to closely supervise your baby when touching small objects to prevent her swallowing or choking on them.

When your baby is holding a small toy, say something like "put it here" and point to where you want her to put it. Gently help her to release her fingers and praise her when the toy is put down.

Standing

Kneel on the floor holding your baby in a standing position facing you. Stand about a foot or two away from her, holding on to her hands. Smile, looking at her face and talking to her, and gradually let go of her hands, keeping yours ready to catch her when she teeters. Watch and mentally note about how many seconds she can stand without holding on. Distract your standing baby from her support by calling to her or waving a toy for her to hold.

Stand in the middle of an area, letting your baby stand and lean with her back against your lower legs, then bend over, holding a toy out in front of her for her to reach for while she stays standing.

Sitting Down

Sit on the floor with your baby and place a toy on the floor. Hold your baby in a standing position as in the previous activity. Let her stand alone and then point to the toy, encouraging her to sit down to get it. You may need to hold her hand(s) and help her lower herself.

13-16 Months

Standing and Stooping

Place a toy on the floor while you stand with your baby. Encourage her to pick it up and give it to you. Watch to see if she bends or stoops to pick it up, then stands again. If she sits, show her how to bend and pick it up, saying "Janie, watch me pick up the ball." Then place her in standing position again and repeat the activity.

Block in Box

Seat your baby on the floor. Place several palm-sized blocks or other safe toys within her reach, along with a shoe box, plastic bowl, dump truck, or other container. Show her how to pick up a block and put it in the box, saying something like "Pick up the block. Put it in." Objects that make a little noise when they're dropped in are more fun.

Throwing

Sit on the floor with your baby. Place several soft, palm-sized balls within her reach. Encourage her to pick one up and throw it by picking one up yourself and throwing it (not at her, but in a direction so she can watch your arm and the ball). As you are encouraging her to throw, be sure to say, "Throw the ball" to emphasize that balls are okay to throw.

Walking

Encourage your baby to walk about the house under supervision. If she reverts to crawling, lift her to standing and walk holding a hand, and then let go, encouraging her to walk on her own. Walk beside her, stopping occasionally and then starting again, and watch to see if she walks with you.

Walking with Variation

Walk around a room beside your child. Walk sideways and encourage her to walk sideways too. If she doesn't, create a narrow passage where she has to walk sideways. Then walk backward beside her, encouraging her to walk backward too.

17-20 Months

Push, Pull, Carry

Place your toddler's hands on the back of a wagon, cart, or three-wheeler. Encourage her to walk and push the wagon. Give your toddler the string to a pull-toy and show her how to walk either forward or backward and pull it. Give her a toy or other object to bring to someone else, encouraging her to walk and carry it, saying, "Give the block to Daddy."

Copycat

Stand facing your toddler and say, "Watch me. Can you do this?" Circle your arms backward and encourage her to watch and do as you do. Try other simple copycat movements like touching your toes, tilting your head from side to side, and kicking your foot.

On and Off

When your toddler is sitting on the floor playing, sit on the sofa facing her. Capture her attention and ask her to come and sit beside you to read a book. Watch to see if she climbs up on her own. Later, get up from the sofa, and then ask her to come to you. Stay close by and watch her climb down. If she is unsure, position her on her tummy so she can scoot off, feet first.

Early Balancing

During dressing, have your toddler stand when it is time to put on her pants. Let her hold on to you as you say, "Lift your foot up," and then guide her foot into her pants leg. Repeat with the other foot.

Walk and Pick Up

Place a palm-sized toy, like a ball, on the floor in the middle of the room. With your toddler across the room from you, say, "Janie, pick up the ball and bring it here." Encourage her to walk to the ball, stoop to pick it up, then continue walking to you.

21-24 Months

Jumping Down

Stand beside your toddler on a low bottom step, holding her hand and facing the floor. Say, "Jump down," and then jump down with both feet, helping her jump down. If she is having trouble, stand facing her, holding both of her hands, and help her jump down.

Kicking a Ball

When outdoors or in a playroom with your toddler, place an 8- to 10-inch ball on the floor in front of you. Kick it gently and say, "Watch, I'm kicking the ball." Then place the ball in front of her and say, "Kick the ball." Praise her when she keeps her balance as she kicks it.

Beginning Running

When outdoors or in a playroom, hold your toddler's hand and say, "Janie, run." Then run forward, holding her hand and encouraging her to run with you. Make it fun by chasing her and letting her chase you. If she falls and is not hurt, don't make a big deal of it, but let her pick herself back up and keep playing.

Standing Up

When your toddler is playing on the floor, ask her to come to you. Watch how she stands up to see if she stands up smoothly and quickly, without falling.

Beginning Throwing

When outdoors or in a playroom, make a target and put it at your toddler's eye level on a wall. With a palm-sized ball, show your toddler how to stand in front of the target and throw the ball overhand at it. A velcro ball and target set work well for this activity, but balls with a lot of bounce should be avoided.

25-30 Months

Upstairs

Place an object or have another person positioned at the top of a staircase. Tell your toddler to walk upstairs while you walk directly behind her for safety. Encourage her to walk up the stairs, holding on to a wall or rail if she wants to. At this stage, she does not need to put one foot on a step, but can put both feet on each step if she wishes.

Jumping Up

Stand facing your toddler and say, "Janie, can you jump like me?" Then jump up and down on both feet in the same place a few times. This activity can be fun when jumping to music, making it a part of "dancing."

Tiptoeing

Show your toddler how to walk on tiptoes. Walk on your tiptoes and say, "Janie, tiptoe, sh-h-h, be quiet." This activity can be fun when playing "surprise" games when you want her to tiptoe up to someone and then surprise them. Tiptoeing is easier to practice and watch for when done on a non-carpeted floor.

Climbing a Jungle Gym

Take your toddler to a playground or facility where a jungle gym is available. (Even many fast food restaurants have them.) Encourage your toddler to climb the apparatus; it is a great exercise for her motor development. Let her navigate as she likes, and watch to see if she can climb up and down on her own.

Walking Backward

Give your toddler a wagon or pull-toy. Show her how to pull the toy and walk backward for a short distance (about 10 feet or more).

31-36 Months

Jumping Forward

Place a string, a rope, or a length of tape on the floor. Have your toddler watch as you jump over it with both feet, then encourage her to jump over the object.

Standing Balance

Stand facing your toddler and tell her to do as you do. Stand on one foot with arms extended shoulder-height to the sides. Say, "Can you stand on one foot like this? Make your arms like an airplane." You may have to hold one or both hands in the beginning. Count to see if she can hold her balance for at least 2 seconds.

Riding a Tricycle

Be sure to start your toddler on a tricycle that is appropriate for her size. She should be able to sit on the seat and comfortably reach the pedals. Place her in position with her feet on the pedals. Push the tricycle slowly forward, holding her in position, so she gets the feel of her feet on the pedals. Gradually let go as she is able to manage it on her own. Then stand about 10 feet away and tell her to pedal to you and stop when she gets there.

Underhand Throwing

Get a large laundry basket or large box to use as a target. Using a palm-sized ball and from about 3 to 5 feet from the basket, show your toddler how to swing her arm and throw the ball underhand into the basket. The goal is not to hit the target, but to show underhand form. Have her watch you, then imitate the throw.

Walking Upstairs

Show your toddler how to walk up the stairs with one foot on each step. Stand on about the fifth or sixth step on a staircase. Tell your toddler to come upstairs to you. Watch to see if she wants to use the handrail. If she does, ask her to do it again, only say, "Can you come up here without holding on?" If you think it is unsafe or that your toddler is not ready, be sure to guide her by holding her hand or by walking behind her. The goal is for her to walk up the steps, one foot on each step, without holding on. Do it again with the full set of stairs.

37-42 Months

Walking Downstairs

Stand at the top of a staircase, holding your preschooler's hand. Say, "Let's walk downstairs," and then slowly walk down the steps, one foot on each step. If she is not ready, let her continue to put two feet on a step for now. When she does it correctly, let her do it again without holding on to your hand.

Catching a Large Ball

Using an 8- to 10-inch lightweight ball, stand about 5 feet away from your preschooler and say, "Let's play catch. Get ready. Watch the ball." Show her how to reach her arms out to catch the ball. Then say, "Catch," and gently toss the ball into her arms. She will probably try unsuccessfully to trap the ball against her body, but eventually she will reach her arms out and successfully catch the ball. After she catches it, have her roll the ball back to you.

Obstacle Course

Set up a safe obstacle course indoors or outdoors where there is ample room to run safely. You can arrange furniture in the living room if the outdoors is not appropriate, or go to a park. Simply play a little game of "chase and catch" and run around the obstacles, telling your preschooler to try and catch you. Lead her through turns going in and out and around things, reminding her not to touch anything. Watch to see if she can follow you without bumping into things.

Hopping

Play a little game of "Simon Says " by asking your preschooler to do what you do. Start with simple movements like circling your arms or touching your toes. Then say, "Simon says hop on one foot," and show her how to hop on one foot in place. Watch to see if she can keep her balance while hopping a couple of times. Then switch feet and see if she can copy you and hop on the other foot.

Balance Beam

Create or find a place to walk on a balance beam. You can create one with a board, or on a safe curb, or on a playground. Play "follow the leader," and get your preschooler to follow you through a simple obstacle course. Add the balance beam while you are playing and show her how to walk on the beam by holding her arms out like an airplane for balance. If she has trouble keeping her balance, help her by holding one of her hands as she walks forward, one foot in front of the other.

43-48 Months

Hopping Forward

Create a pattern on the floor or outdoors on a sidewalk by placing five circles or squares about 6 inches apart in a row. Tell your preschooler to watch you as you hop on one foot from one spot to another, keeping your other foot up and your arms out for balance. Then say, "Now you try." She may have to hop once, then put her foot down before she hops again, but keep playing to see if she can hop more than two hops in a row without putting her foot down.

Bounce Catch

Use an 8- to 10-inch rubber ball and stand 6 to 10 feet away from your preschooler. Tell her to get ready to catch the ball by putting her arms out. Then bounce the ball gently so it bounces up to her waist or chest height. Tell her to throw or roll the ball back to you, then keep bouncing it to her until she catches it. If she is having trouble, stand a little closer, then increase the distance gradually.

Galloping

Play some lively music and tell your preschooler to ride her "horse." Then show her how to gallop leading with one foot and following with the other. Holding your arms like you're riding a horse, say "Giddyup." Then encompass the gallop in a game of "follow the leader," and combine it with running, hopping, walking backward and sideways.

Heel-Toe

Use wide masking tape to put a straight line about 6 feet long on the floor. Then show your preschooler how to walk on the line with the heel of one foot touching the toe of the other foot, putting your arms out for balance. Help her at first by holding her hand while she does it. Then make a game of it and tell your preschooler that there are alligators around the line and that you must walk on the line. Be sure to make it fun without scaring her.

Jumping Over

Place a shoestring, tissue, or stick on the floor and tell your preschooler to jump over it like you do. Show her how to jump with both feet at the same time and then have her try. You can create a little obstacle course by placing several objects about the room, and then play "follow the leader," leading her through the course and jumping safely over the objects.

49-60 Months

Catching with Hands

Using an 8- to 10-inch ball, stand about 6 feet from your preschooler and tell her to get ready to catch the ball with her hands by putting her arms out. Then gently toss the ball to her and say, "Catch the ball with your hands." She may trap the ball against her body, but keep trying and show her how her hands should catch the ball on each side.

Tiptoe Balance

Ask your preschooler to stand really tall on her tiptoes and show her how to keep her balance by extending her arms. Tell her you're going to count to see how long she can stand on her tiptoes, then go ahead and count as she tries. Praise her and see if she can hold her balance for the count of 10.

Jumping Up and Over

Find an object at your child's knee level for your preschooler to jump over. You can use a loosely held jump rope, a stack of paperback books, or a yardstick resting loosely on two surfaces. Show your preschooler how to stand on one side with feet together and knees bent. Then jump over the obstacle with both feet together. Tell your preschooler to jump, and hold her hand the first time. If she seems ready, let her try it on her own as you watch for her safety. Stress that she should swing her arms to help her jump.

Backward Heel-Toe

Create a 2-inch-wide line on the floor about 10 feet long. Show your preschooler how to walk backward on the line with the toe of one foot touching the heel of the other one, while holding your arms out for balance. Hold your preschooler's hand as she tries it, then gradually let go to see if she can keep her balance.

Hop-a-Long

Stand on one side of a room while your preschooler is facing you on the other. Tell her to watch you hop on one foot across the room (be sure to hop at least six times). Show her how to use her arms to help her hop. Then tell her to try to hop all the way across.

61-72 Months

Skipping

Skipping is fun to do to lively music. With the music on, show your child how to skip alternating feet. When it's her turn to try, she might gallop at first. Tell her to step-hop with one foot, then step-hop with the other, and sing "Skip to My Lou."

Toe Touch

As a morning wake-up exercise, tell your daughter that she should stretch, reach her hands straight above her head, then bend over with straight or slightly bent legs and try to touch her toes. Show her how, then do about 10 with her. If she can't reach her toes, tell her to reach down as far as she can.

Bike Riding

A two-wheel bike with training wheels is a good way for a child to get the feel of the bike. Begin with the training wheels close to the ground, and as she progresses, gradually raise the training wheels so she gets the feeling of balancing the bike. At first, walk along beside her, supporting her and the bike, and slowly push it forward, as she gets the feel of the balance and motion of the pedals.

One-Hand Bounce-Catch

Use a tennis ball or similar rubber ball with a good bounce that's the size of a child's hand. On a hard surface, show your child how to bounce the ball in front of you so it hits the floor once, and then catch it in one hand. Let your child try it; count with her to see how many times she can bounce and catch the ball while standing in place.

10-Second Balance

Mark a spot on a floor with a hard surface. Show your child how to stand on the spot with one foot, hold the other foot up, hold arms out to the sides, look straight ahead, and hold the balance for a count of 10. Then let her try it. If she has trouble at first, hold one hand and gradually let go as her balance improves.

8

Activities to Enhance Communicating

It is often said that children develop in spite of our well-intentioned teaching. Often, all we really need to do is to provide ample chances for our children to explore on their own. Below is a laundry list of communication-based activities to introduce to your son or daughter. Consider the list a springboard from which you can launch into your own ideas for enhancing your child's development. Take the ideas listed below and make them work for you, for your child, and for your family. While some ideas may seem simplistic and repetitive, they are perfect for most children. If your child wants to do the same thing over and over, that is perfectly normal and should be encouraged. If your child turns away, struggles, resists, or otherwise indicates she doesn't want to participate, listen to her. Children are notorious for disliking something once, then adoring it the next time, so don't give up— try, try again.

Play is "child's work" and your baby should spend much of her waking alert times in some sort of play. While the play activities listed below are organized into developmental categories, it is important to remember that play in one area develops all areas.

It is important to allow and encourage your child to explore her environment with as much independence and self-motivation as is safe for her age. As your child grows, her need for your supervision, direction, and motivation will vary. You might come to realize that your child resists your attempts to "teach" her. Listen to her. Allow her to explore and learn on her own. Provide the materials and the opportunity. While this independence is important, your child

should never be completely unsupervised or allowed to use toys, tools or appliances not intended for children her chronological or developmental age.

The most important principle in enhancing language development is experience. You must let your child listen to and make a variety of sounds as she explores her environment. Parents who interrupt their babies do not listen, respond, or give them a chance to vocalize, thus impeding their children's language growth and development. From the earliest stages in infancy, respond to your baby's gurgles, coos, babbles, and cries. Talk to her a lot—when you are dressing her, changing her, feeding her, and playing with her. As she becomes a toddler and her language skills grow, you will be amazed at the words and sentences she adds to her vocabulary. Your role is to provide a vocabulary-rich environment. Reading books, listening to stories on tapes, visiting new environments, and talking about what she sees—all are experiences that enhance language.

The activities below link directly to the items in the checklist. If your child has scored "low" on a particular language behavior that you think she should be able to do, study the activity in the list below and incorporate it into your child's routine. Feel free to adapt or expand the activity to suit your home and situation. Most of all, have fun with these activities! Although they are designed to practice and reinforce specific aspects of language, they cannot be successful until they're brought to life; only you can make the learning process fun.

0-4 Months

Cooing and Babbling

When your baby is content and alert, prop her on your lap or in an infant seat so she is facing you. Talk to her in a pleasant voice. Capture her attention and see if she responds with coos and babbles. When she does, continue the "conversation" with her. Talk to her during daily activities too, such as during diaper-changing, feeding, and dressing.

Talk to your baby at every opportunity. Tell her everything you are doing to her and for her, like "Janie needs a diaper change. I'm going to change your diaper. Here we go, I'm taking your diaper off. Does it feel cold? Lets clean you up. Here comes the clean diaper. Doesn't that feel good?" Talk all the time about everything you are doing.

Encourage your baby's noises by responding to all of them. Respond to her noises by talking back to her about anything you think she might be "commenting" on. Respond to her sounds by feeding her, changing her diaper, and cuddling, patting, and tickling her.

Talk face-to-face with your baby. Look into her eyes from a distance of 10 to 12 inches away.

Imitate your baby's noises and encourage her coos and babbles by talking to her. Make all kinds of sounds while looking at your baby. Be sure to repeat words and sounds that seem to attract her attention or please her.

Vowel Sounds

Listen carefully to your baby's coos and babbles. Note whether she makes any of the vowel sounds (a, e, i, o, or u). The sounds can be *ah, oh, uh,* and similar sounds. When she is facing you and alert, talk to her in a pleasant voice and see if you can stimulate her to talk to you with some vowel sounds.

Laughing

During dressing or when she is alert and content, capture her attention by talking to her in a pleasant voice. Make noises, sing, "blow" on her tummy, and try other interactions to see if she smiles and laughs out loud.

Listening

When your baby is awake and not crying while in her crib or playpen in a quiet room, watch her reaction as you walk in and talk to her as you approach. If she turns her head toward you, or otherwise shows she is listening to you, she is responding to your voice. Try it again by approaching her from another direction.

Smile and talk right to your baby's face so she can easily see you, to encourage her listening.

Prop toys up so your baby can knock them over, then praise her efforts and reward her by giving her the toy. Talk to her about the toys and make your voice sound excited when she knocks them over, to encourage her listening.

Attention-Seeking

When your baby is content and alert, move away from her so you're at least 10 feet away, and see if she makes sounds to capture your attention. Note whether she coos, babbles, gurgles, cries, or makes other noises purposely to get you to come to her. This early step shows that your baby is learning that making noise can accomplish a goal.

Respond to your baby's noises and movements. If she startles or jerks, ask her if she is surprised. If she kicks or flails her arms, ask her what it is she is trying to get. Guess at what it is she is responding to and bring it closer for her to inspect. Pick her up, move closer to her, and call to her so that she learns that her sounds and movements will get you to pay attention.

5-8 Months

Making Connected Sounds

When your baby is content and alert, talk to her. See if she makes three or more sounds in one breath, like "ba-ba-ba," or "da-ba-ka." If she doesn't, make those sounds yourself and see if she tries to repeat them. These connected sounds are important first steps toward connected speech.

Let your baby coo and babble to your face, but try not to interrupt during daily activities while she "talks."

Make all kinds of sounds for your baby to imitate like "dadadadada," "babababababa," "mamamama," etc.

Making Different Sounds

Listen carefully to your baby's speech. Does she make more than one sound like "da" and "ba"? These don't have to be successive or in the same breath, just any two different syllables. "Ka," "ma," and "mu" are common sounds babies make at this age. If she only makes one, then you should continue to talk to her and make different sounds to stimulate a variety in the sounds she makes.

Make both loud and soft sounds for your baby to hear, and listen intently when she responds.

First Syllables

Listen to see if your baby makes the sounds of at least two syllables. The syllable sounds your baby makes don't need to be the same—she may say "da-ba," or "da-ba-ka," or "da-da-da," and she would still pass this milestone. The point of this activity is that the sounds are made successively. Once again, talk with your baby when you have her attention, and encourage her to "talk" with you.

Name Recognition

When your baby is propped up, content, and alert, be casually present in the room talking but not using her name. Then say her name, and see if she responds to it. She will look directly at you, listen, smile, or quiet her activity when she recognizes it. If she doesn't react to it, then begin to emphasize it with a higher pitch or different tone in your voice.

Call your baby by her name, then go to her to give her something or play with her.

Change the words to common children's songs and rhymes to silly things that include your baby's name, and when you sing or say her name poke or tickle her.

Ask your baby where she is, "Where's Janie?" pause and, with a little poke, say "Here you are! Here's Janie!"

Use your baby's name frequently when playing with and talking to her.

Shouting

When your baby is playing, cooing, and babbling, note whether she raises her voice. She may actually shout her babbles. If she doesn't, then vary your own loudness level and make your conversations more animated. Varying loudness is an important step toward developing the variety of sounds in natural language.

9-12 Months

Imitating Sounds

When you are talking with your baby, make some definite, distinct sounds for her to imitate. For example, say "buh," "da," "ma," or actual common words like *milk, Daddy, bye-bye,* or other simple sounds and words to see if she will try to imitate you. Present only one word or sound at a time and repeat it.

Make sounds while looking into your baby's eyes from a distance of 12 to 18 inches away. Make one sound, pause, then show pleasure at any response your baby makes. When your baby imitates your sounds, show a little more pleasure and excitement. Say something like "You sound just like me, aren't you a smart girl?"

Recognizing Words

When your baby is playing and is content, talk to other family members or to her and use familiar words like *outside, car, dog, naptime,* or *eat.* Note whether she seems to recognize these words by turning her attention to you, or "talking" back to you. When she pauses or looks up, acknowledge what she heard by saying something like "You are right, I said bye-bye." If your baby is not yet paying attention to familiar words, call her name, get her attention, and repeat the word. Show her a familiar object and repeat the name of the object. Good words might include *bottle, Mommy, Daddy, no, baby, walk, park,* and names of toys.

Saying "No"

When you are feeding your baby and she does not want to eat certain foods, note whether she says "no" and shakes her head. If she doesn't, ask her "No?"

and shake your head. When she is into something she shouldn't be into, then say "no," shake your head, and lead her away from the object.

Whenever you say "no," shake your head. Repeat no, shaking your head. Make sure your baby can see you shake your head and hear you say no. When she shakes her head, say "no" until she starts to say it for herself. When she says "no," agree with her by saying "no" and shaking your head.

First Words

When you are conversing with your baby and she says a word that has a meaning that you understand, repeat it and smile. For example, if she points to a bird and says "birdie" or a word close to the word "birdie," smile, point to the bird, and say, "Yes, Janie, look at the birdie." Make a big deal out of these words, so she will continue to use them. At this point, you want her to say at least two words that you understand. You can reinforce this by clearly labeling common objects, like *cookie, kitty, bye-bye,* and *ball.* Don't be concerned if no one else understands what your baby is saying as long as you do.

Encourage your baby to repeat words you say. Look her in the eye and say something like "bottle," then say "Now you say bottle," then pause, and when she makes a noise, say something like "yes, bottle."

Using Names

Emphasize the names of people in the household, and see if your baby can say them. She may babble names like "Zuda" for *Susie,* "Da" for *Daddy,* or "Momma-ma" for *Mommy.* If she doesn't, be sure to stress the names and point to each person and try to get her to repeat the names. When she does say them, reinforce it, by saying, "Yes, that's Daddy."

Ask your baby, "Where is Mama, where is Dada?" In your family *Mama* and *Dada* may be *Mom, Dad, Grandma, Aunt, Papa,* or whatever family names are given or used for the most important caretakers of your baby.

13-16 Months

New Words

Pay attention to your baby's speech. It may sound like babbles, but many of those babbles may actually be attempts at words. Keep a notebook available and jot down recognizable words or those sounds she uses like words. She should be saying at least four words by now. When she does say a word, reinforce it by repeating it and pointing to the object or person. Have other members of the household carry on conversations with her and listen to her speech. Have them tell you words they clearly heard and understood.

Repeat words that your baby is trying to say. Avoid drawing attention to her mispronunciations—simply let her hear you say the word correctly. When she talks to others, say something like "That's good, you asked grandma for a cookie," rather than speaking for your baby.

Following Directions

It's important that your baby be able to follow simple commands. Start at a very early age with simple directions like "Go and pick up the ball," "Shut the door," or "Bring me the book." When she does the action correctly, be sure to reinforce it immediately by saying, "Good, Janie, you picked up the ball. Thank you."

Start by giving simple directions like "Get the truck," repeat it, then lead her to the truck, and tell her "Pick it up" and "Give it to me." Show your enthusiasm when she does any part of the direction without your help.

Expressing Ideas

As your baby is participating in the world around her, note whether she begins to initiate her own observations. For example, she might say, "Daddy is eating." If she doesn't seem to be initiating, then you must make a deliberate attempt at making observational comments like "It's cold outside" or "The cookies are all gone" or "Where's the truck?" and encourage her to repeat them.

Talk to your baby, telling her about things she sees and does. Pick out one word from your description and say it again, like "I am washing your face, washing. Can you say washing?" If she approximates the word, say "yes," and repeat it again. When your baby points to something and says something, repeat a word that seems to fit the situation. Try to figure out what your baby is trying to tell you.

Naming Wants

When you think your baby wants something like a cracker, hold up the cracker to her and say, "Do you want a cracker?" Try to encourage her to say the word *cracker.* Look for other opportunities for her to use a key word to express her wants, like *bottle, book,* or *cookie.*

Each time your baby points to something, name it for her, ask her to say it, then repeat the word.

Making Up Words

Note whether your baby has invented special words for people or things. For example, she may say "booda" for *blanket* or "coco" for *cookie.* When she does use them, simply acknowledge that you know what she is talking about, get the object, and then say the correct word for it.

Listen to your baby's words and repeat them however she says them. Ask her what it means, where it is, to point to it, or show it to you, then repeat her word for the item or event. Do this with words you hear her say often.

17-20 Months

Listening for 3 Minutes

In a quiet room, read a story or play an audio recording that your toddler chooses to note whether you can hold her attention for at least 3 minutes. It's a good idea to read stories to your baby regularly. Read the stories with interest and make them fun. Stop at certain pages and point out animals, objects, and people, so she really looks at the page and learns new words.

Read to your toddler for at least 20 minutes each day. This time might be spread out over many sessions and can include reading signs and cereal boxes or parts of books she sees you reading. Start with phrases, rhymes, jingles, or very short stories. String two of these sessions together, building to longer and longer reading sessions.

Ten or More Words

You or another family member should engage your toddler in conversations throughout a day or two. With a notepad or tape recorder available, jot down or record all the recognizable words your toddler uses. At this age, your toddler should spontaneously say 10 or more words. If she doesn't, keep reading her stories, talk more throughout the day, and point to people, animals, and things while clearly labeling them and encouraging your toddler to repeat the words.

Play "Word Safari." Walk through your home with your toddler, pointing to and naming the things she sees. Write down the words she uses as she names things, so that she can see as you write. Ask questions about the things she says to get her to use different words. At the end of your safari, read her the list of words that she used while she looks on. Date the list and do it again a week or so later, adding only the new words she uses.

Talking into a Play Phone

A plastic play phone is a terrific toy for your toddler. If your toddler does not have a play phone, use an unused real phone that she can manipulate safely and comfortably. You should pick up the receiver, pretend to dial, and then talk into the phone like it's a real conversation. Then let her do it. Emphasize saying "Hello" and "Good-bye" at the beginning and end of the conversation.

Make a play phone from a paper towel roll or pieces of cardboard. Or give your toddler a discarded, real phone with the cords removed. Pretend to call your toddler, making ringing sounds, answering hello, asking her name and how she is, and then saying good-bye and hanging up. Tell her to call you.

Answering Questions

When you are conversing with your toddler, ask her different questions. You can ask, "Where is Mommy today?" or "Do you want something to drink?" or "Where is your cap?" Be sure to wait for an answer, and if she does answer, follow through by giving her something to drink or saying, "Yes, Mommy's at work and will be home later."

Start by asking your toddler "yes" and "no" questions: "Do you want a cookie?" Repeat her response, either yes or no. If she doesn't respond, ask again, if she doesn't respond, then answer for her either yes or no. For example, ask her, "Do you want to read a book?" and again, "Do you want to read a book? Yes, you want to read a book," then read the book. Once your toddler is responding to "yes/no" questions, move to questions that can be answered with words or gestures, like "Where is Auntie?" If your child doesn't respond, give her the answer by pointing and saying something like "There is Auntie" or "Auntie is at work" and point to the door, or "Auntie is bye-bye" and wave.

Naming Objects

Play "What's that?" by pointing to objects throughout your home or in a store or outdoors. When she names something correctly, say "Yes, that's a flower." When she is wrong or doesn't know, point to the object, tell her the name, and get her to repeat the word. She should be able to name most familiar objects.

21-24 Months

Twenty or More Words

Build on the recording of your child's vocabulary. Keep the list out where it's handy or have the tape recorder available to record her new words. At this point, she should spontaneously say at least 20 words. If not, get more books and keep reading to your toddler on a daily basis. Have her repeat words to you and keep labeling objects seen on TV and in her environment. Praise her when she does say a new word.

Place a voice-activated tape recorder in a safe place near where your toddler plays and in her room at night. Do this for a few days, then count the number of words she uses. Let her listen to herself talk and point to the objects she names on the tape.

Knowing First Name

On a regular basis, at least several times a week, ask your toddler, "What's your name?" Then say her first name and have her repeat it. Have other people ask her name and encourage her to say it.

Call your toddler by her name often. Ask your toddler what her name is, and pause. If she does not respond, say something like "Your name is Mary," then repeat the question. Respond enthusiastically to any attempt she makes to say her own name, then repeat her name for her. Listen and look for your toddler's name in other places and say things like "There is another girl who is named Mary" or "You and Auntie are both named Mary."

Imitating Words

You can really help your toddler build her vocabulary at this age. Tell her new words all the time and encourage her to copy them and say them back to you. Don't hold back on big words like *elevator*—she may actually remember them even better. Try to introduce a couple of new words every day. Take your toddler with you to environments outside of your home. The grocery store, the doctor's office, or the gas station can provide rich opportunities for expanding her vocabulary.

Name the things you use and describe the things you are doing with new words. Say these words while your toddler can see your lips move from straight ahead. Encourage her imitation of your words by taking the time to repeat words. Resist correcting her pronunciation— simply repeat the word for her to imitate, then move on to another word.

Rhymes

Sing-song rhymes are fun and inviting to your toddler at this age. Use a Mother Goose, Dr. Seuss, or other colorful rhyme book and read the same rhymes to her over and over. Encourage her to say them along with you. Then, at a later time, see if she can say one or two lines on her own, or see if she can finish it when you've started the rhyme.

Include a rhyme in the form of a song, jingle, or prayer in different parts of your toddler's routine. Use something like "Humpty Dumpty sat on a wall, Humpty Dumpty had a great fall" for when she cries; "Hickory, dickory dock, the mouse ran up the clock" for bedtimes; or "God is great, God is good" for meal times. Soon your toddler will be saying it with you.

Two-Word Sentences

Now your toddler is connecting her speech into two-word sentences. See if she uses two words to communicate an idea, like "Go bye-bye" or "Daddy home."

If she is still saying single words, try to extend them into simple sentences and get her to repeat them. For example, if she says "cookie," you say "Does Janie want a cookie?" and repeat the words "want cookie," then encourage her to repeat it.

Use three- and four-word sentences with your toddler. When she uses one word to express herself, wait expectantly, looking into your toddler's eyes for another word. At first, supply her with another word. As she begins to add another word or gesture, say the two words together. Something like "water" is repeated "Water? Water there? Yes, water is there."

25-30 Months

Imitating Parents

When you are playing with your toddler, building blocks or reading a book, change the tone of your voice, and see if she imitates your tone. For example, say excitedly, "Oooh, that's a big tower!" or sadly, "Oh-oh, it all fell down," or angrily, "Bad behavior, kitty!"

Talk to others in front of your toddler with expression in your voice, face, and body. Keep her nearby so that she can see your responses and reactions to all sorts of things that you encounter in your day —songs on the radio, TV programs, conversations with others, sales calls, other drivers, and so forth. When your toddler imitates you in any way, say something like "That is what I do, isn't it," then ask her how she would say it. Re-enact your tone of voice for her so she can imitate it. Encourage appropriate imitation of your tone of voice in her play with her toys by laughing and commenting how she sounds "just like me!"

Songs and Rhymes

Sing-song rhymes and funny songs are stimulating to your toddler at this age. Get books like Bill Martin's *Brown Bear, Brown Bear;* Margaret Wise Brown's *Good Night Moon*, or other colorful rhyming books and read them to her. Encourage her to say the rhymes along with you. Then, at a later time, see if she repeats parts (more than two lines) of the songs or rhymes on her own.

Sing the same few songs or rhymes your toddler chooses every night before going to bed. Have her ask for the song or rhyme by name and repeat it for her.

Three-Word Sentences

You can help your toddler become a better communicator by encouraging her to string more than two words together for a sentence. For example, she may say, "Daddy home." You can say, "Daddy's coming home," and encourage her to repeat the three words. Or she may say, "Fido outside," and you say, "Fido is playing outside."

I, You, and Me

In her ever-expanding vocabulary, encourage your toddler to use the personal pronouns *I, you,* and *me.* If she says to her father, "Daddy want apple?" you can look at Daddy and say, "Do you want an apple?" and encourage her to repeat the question with the word *you.* Find other opportunities to reinforce use of the pronouns *I, you,* and *me.*

When your toddler expresses herself, repeat her sentences adding *I, you,* and *me.* At meal times try saying things like "I like peanut butter, Daddy likes peanut butter, you like peanut butter." When your toddler brings you things, exclaim "For me?"

Asking Questions

It may really try your patience when your toddler relentlessly asks questions. But it's important that you answer her questions as much as possible.

Encourage your toddler's questions by answering them. If you don't know the answer, say something like "I don't know, but maybe Mommy knows. Let's ask Mommy" or "Let's look for the answer in that book." If your toddler seems reluctant to ask questions, point out things that might be curious to her, like "Look at that man with one shoe" or "Look at all of this dirt."

31-36 Months

Conversations

Make general comments to your preschooler, like "You are playing with your dinosaurs," and pause to give her the chance to respond. If she responds, make another brief logical statement or ask a question about dinosaurs or her play and wait for her response. Continue until she loses interest in the conversation. If she does not respond, ask a question. At first, if your toddler responds about something that is unrelated, change the conversation to her topic making statements and asking questions. Count the number of logical statements and responses made by your toddler and increase your questioning slowly. If possible, try to ignore responses that are completely off the topic, and repeat your question or statement.

Have a "tea party" or "juice break" with your toddler. Sit down at a table with your toddler and engage her in a conversation. Ask her questions and see if she answers you. Pause and give her the opportunity to make a comment on her own. Note whether there is clearly a verbal give and take. It need only be brief, but it should take the form of a logical conversation.

Who, Where, and When?

During a conversation with your toddler, like during the "tea party" described above, ask her *who* questions, *where* questions, and *when* questions. Give her time to answer, and if she doesn't, ask again and then help her with the answer.

Read a short, simple story to your preschooler, then turn back to the beginning, reread one page at a time, and ask appropriate "who, where, and when" questions.

Monthly Vocabulary Explosion

Although you may not be able to count the number of new words your toddler is using each month, take notice of the variety of new words your toddler uses. At this stage, the number of new words should be amazing to you. Actually, she should be adding about 50 words each month, though you will no longer be counting them. If you feel she is not adding new words, spend more time reading to your toddler, engaging her in conversation, and simply involving her in as much verbal activity as possible.

Make a list of all the words your preschooler uses. Keep the list handy as you interact with her throughout the day. Add to your list, over a couple of days. Draw a heavy line after the last word, or number the list then put it away for a month or two. Repeat the activity, and count the words. Read the list to your preschooler and ask her if there are other words she uses. Talk about the words on the list.

"What to Do" Questions

During play, ask your toddler "What do you do when . . ." questions. For example, ask "What do you do when you are sleepy?" Then wait for the appropriate answer, "I go to bed." Other questions to ask include "What do you do when you are thirsty?" and "What do you do when you are hungry?"

Tell your preschooler when she looks or acts thirsty, hungry, sleepy, crabby, happy, or angry, and tell her why she looks that way. Say something like "Foot stomping makes you look angry, are you?" or "You get a drink when you are thirsty. Tell me what you do when you are hungry or sleepy or tired." When she asks for a drink, say something like "When you are thirsty, you get a drink." Finally, ask her what she should do when she is sleepy, tired, crabby, happy, and so forth.

Using Prepositions and Directional Words

Place several blocks and other toys on the floor and sit among them with your toddler. Ask your toddler to perform several tasks with the blocks. You might say, "Put the dinosaur *on* the box," or "Put the ball *in* the bucket" or "*Empty* the box. Now the box is *empty*" or "Put the toys *in* the box. Now the box is *full*." You'll want to observe your toddler's understanding of the relationship among the objects.

Play with these words by using a bowl and some small toys. Ask your preschooler to fill the bowl with the toys, then exclaim "all full"; tell her to dump the bowl, then exclaim "empty" and so on. Once she is good at demonstrating *in, on, empty,* and *full,* change places and have her tell you what to do. Occasionally, do it wrong, and let her correct you.

37-42 Months

Talking Clearly

Start a conversation with your preschooler. If she babbles or mispronounces certain words, say the word(s) correctly, and have her repeat after you. At this point, she should say most words clearly enough for you and most anyone else to understand.

Give your preschooler plenty of opportunities to talk with you, other family members, and friends. Avoid speaking for her, allowing her to explain for herself. Repeat words her audience doesn't hear or understand, and ask questions.

Talking About Pictures

Show your preschooler snapshots, magazine pictures, or pictures in a book. Slowly look at each page and ask her what is happening in the picture. Wait for her to describe in her own words what is happening. Share what you think and why you think it.

Keep magazines, picture books, and photo albums handy for your preschooler to look at. Ask her what is happening in the various pictures, then have her draw her own pictures and tell you about them.

Using Plurals

At early stages, children do not use plurals when they are talking. At 37 to 42 months, your preschooler should begin to add the "s" ending to all words to indicate plurals. For example, she should say *blocks* when referring to a pile of blocks, rather than the singular, *block*. She may not be ready to use irregular plurals, and may add the "s" ending to words to indicate more than one (for example, she may say "mouses" instead of mice, or "sheeps" instead of sheep).

Use plurals when talking to your preschooler. Talk about things in groups. Ask her to name groups of things that you see. If she uses the singular, repeat her answer in the plural form. Avoid correcting her irregular plurals. Say something like "Yes, that picture shows more than one mouse; it shows some mice," or "Yes, there are three mice in that picture."

Using the *and* a

Your preschooler's sentences should begin to sound less like "preschooler talk" and more complete. Engage your preschooler in a conversation. When she omits the words *the* or *a,* repeat the statement as it should be. For example, when she says, "I want cracker," you say, "Do you want *a* cracker?" Read your toddler books and sing her songs with sentences and lyrics containing *the* and *a.*

Mastering Songs and Rhymes

Using a Mother Goose, Dr. Seuss, or other book of songs or rhymes, pick several of your preschooler's favorites to teach her. Repeat the selected rhyme and have her say it with you. Then let her say it by herself. Songs and rhymes like "London Bridge," "Rock-a-Bye Baby," Happy Birthday," "Humpty-Dumpty," "Rain, Rain, Go Away," and "Hickory Dickory Dock" all work well at this age. Listen to see if she knows all the words. If she wants it, give her help when she gets stuck.

Sing whole songs to your preschooler, repeating the same song for a few days until she can sing along with you. Then start her singing the same song, while you sing along more softly. Sing the song with the wrong words and let your preschooler correct you. Finally, let her sing the song without you.

43-48 Months

Imagining

Encourage your preschooler to create imaginary situations. Playing make believe is important for your preschooler's overall development. For example, let her build a tent under the table and pretend it's a house and talk about what is happening. Let her dress up in office clothes and pretend she's at the office. Let her talk about pretend situations and play along with her. Let her bring out the preschooler in you and let her see that it's okay to imagine.

Storytime

Continue to read stories to your preschooler. Try to read in a quiet room without distractions. Begin to read longer stories, increasing the length of time you read by a few minutes each day until you hold your preschooler's attention for at least 20 minutes. Always keep the stories interesting with your voice. Let her ask questions and discuss the pictures.

Choose longer and longer books to read to your preschooler. Continue to read a longer book until your preschooler begins to squirm or look around, then read one more sentence, brief page or paragraph. Tell stories about your preschooler's infancy, lengthening the story with more and more details, including your feelings and what everyone did and said in relationship to your preschooler when she was a baby.

Word Play

Your preschooler may giggle and laugh as she makes up her own words for fun. Encourage her to do so and laugh along with her. Word play shows your preschooler's developing understanding of language. "Dad, that's a tork, not a fork," or "Grandma, I want a chocanookie" or "Mom, it's so big, it's huge-a-tiffic," are examples of ways your preschooler might make up new words.

Make up some words of your own. Talk about being so angry you "scrupled and criddled," then laugh. Tell your preschooler you are going to "smickle" her. Explain a familiar task using made-up silly words. Describe a situation and have your preschooler make up some of the words for you.

Expressing Feelings

Using children's stories, stop and discuss feelings when there's an opportunity. Talk about sad, happy, excited, frustrated, and angry feelings. Use feeling words when real situations arise with members of the family. "Tommy is sad right now; he is crying. Can you make him feel better?" It's also a good idea for your preschooler to see that you have feelings too. When you are frustrated, tell her, "I feel frustrated right now, because . . ." Encourage her to use feeling words. Realize that she may only be able to use four or five words to express her feelings, but it's better than acting out or keeping it in.

Describe your feelings around your preschooler frequently, saying things like "I am angry right now" or "That makes me so happy" or "I'm so excited for Grandma to come, I can't wait." Comment on what you think others are feeling and why. Say things like "She looks afraid" or "Daddy must be frustrated— he's jumping up and down" or "Her tears tell me she is sad." Name your preschooler's emotions and describe why you think she is feeling that way. Ask your preschooler questions like "Does that picture make you feel cozy?" or "Does that game confuse you?" or "That is really a hard thing—are you frustrated?"

Silly Rhyming

Your preschooler should giggle and take delight in creating silly rhymes. Encourage her imagination, laugh and play along. Try changing the words to a familiar holiday song into a silly rhyme, like "Jingle bells, Batman smells, Robin laid an egg." The words might make little or no sense and the phrases be ridiculous, but your preschooler should show continued interest in what she can do with words.

Rhyme all sorts of words, even making up silly words for your preschooler. Tell her to try, then give her a word to rhyme. Recite things like "see ya later alligator," "not so soon ya big baboon," and "after while crocodile." Change the words to songs like "Rock-A-Bye Baby," "Hush Little Baby," and "Twinkle, Twinkle Little Star" to silly rhymes and situations.

49-60 Months

First and Last Names

On a regular basis, ask your preschooler her name. If she says her first name, tell her her first and last names and have her repeat them. Keep practicing until she automatically says her first and last names clearly. Have other people she knows ask her her name so she is comfortable telling people.

While driving or riding places, repeat in sing-song your child's whole name. Have her take a turn. Use her complete name in a story where you repeat it throughout the story, pausing each time you are about to repeat her name and having her say it with you.

Arguing

A real sign of maturation is your preschooler's use of words to argue. Up to this point, your preschooler may have had tantrums, or cried when in an argument. At this stage, when you see that she needs to make a point, encourage her to slow down, take a breath, and then talk to whomever she is arguing with. Tell her to stop and listen to the other person, and then to tell her side. Let her know that physical outbursts are not acceptable. When she is arguing with you, and does express herself verbally, reinforce her argument by saying, "Yes, Janie, I hear that you are not happy about staying inside. Thank you for telling me. Now, what else can we do?"

Encourage your child to use words to fight. Say things like "Tell me what you want," or "Tell others no," or "Scream or shout or move away from others who make you angry." When your child does not want to do something, ask her why and listen patiently. Reward her use of words by listening intently, respecting what she has to say, and compromising your position if appropriate.

Joking

At this stage, encourage your preschooler's attempts at silly jokes. They may not make sense to you, but if she shows she thinks they're funny, play along.

It's important for her to develop her sense of humor. She might say something like "Knock, knock. Who's there? Underwear."

Get a children's joke book and read it to your toddler. When others visit, ask her something like "What was that joke about the pumpkin?"

Five-Word Sentences

Engage your preschooler in conversation during a quiet play time or at the dinner table. Tape-record or make note of her sentences, which should be of five or six words, or more. If they are not this long, continue to carry on conversations with your preschooler and read stories, encouraging longer sentences during your conversations. Repeat her sentences, adding words to show you understand what she is thinking about.

Let your child use a tape recorder to record her own stories. Listen to the tape with your child, pausing the tape to repeat sentences and add a few words to them. Talk to your child in longer and longer sentences.

Basic Sounds

Choose a new picture book or story to read together. As you read the story, stop and look at the pictures and enter into a conversation with your preschooler. Have a tape recorder or notepad ready, and make note of sounds in words that are mispronounced. At this stage, the "b, p, m, w, h, d, t, n, g, k, ng, y" sounds should be made correctly. These sounds may fall anywhere in the word. Good words to try are: *bug, put, mom, we, have, dog, cat, song,* and *yes.* If you discover that your preschooler is mispronouncing any of these sounds, make note of it, then model the correct sound to her using a variety of words.

Get pictures of items with difficult sounds in them. Have your child name the items, noting which sounds she makes clearly and correctly. Repeat the words she uses. The beginning sounds she does not make can be practiced by repeating the sound a few times in a row, then saying the rest of the word. Have her guess what you are going to say by giving only part of the word.

61-72 Months

Name and Address

Several times a week, even daily, ask your child her name and address. She should be able to clearly recite her first and last name, her address, and her age. If she stumbles, help her and have her repeat the sequence correctly.

Repeat your child's full name, age, and address in a sing-song voice, having your child repeat part by part. As she learns each part, add another part. Ask things like "Who lives at (address)?" and require her to say her whole name, followed by her age. Require your child to recite her whole name and address or parts of her address as she learns it before she gets to go play, gets out of the car, or has a treat.

Feelings

Ask short, simple questions to encourage your child to talk about her feelings, for example, "How did that make you feel?" Listen for answers of two to three sentences or longer. If she has trouble describing her feelings, help her out by asking her, "Do you feel _____? Tell me why you feel that way." Model the discussion by telling her about your feelings when the opportunity arises.

Use your child's words and expressions to ask about her feelings. After she responds, say something like "Tell me more" or "What else?"

Beginning Sounds

An awareness of beginning sounds in words is important for school-bound children. Say some words and have your child repeat the word. Repeat the beginning sound in the same word a few times and have your child copy you. Comment about what sound that is. Concentrate on beginning sounds, not beginning letters.

Use picture books, and identify familiar objects and animals. Tell her, for example, "Bear begins with 'buh.' What else begins with this sound?" You might want to work on one sound a day and make a game out of it. "How many things begin with an s-s-s-s sound?"

Well-Constructed Sentences

Use well-constructed sentences when you talk. Help her use nouns and verb tenses correctly. Her sentences should usually follow traditional rules of grammar, showing emerging sophistication with language—her sentences should sound correct. Practice by carrying on extended high-interest conversations with your child.

Have your child watch TV programs and listen to radio programs that use language properly. Practice with your child.

Sharing

When you have company or are in the presence of others, have your child share her experiences. Encourage her to describe some of her recent activities. Prompt her by saying things like "Oh, Grandma, just wait until you hear what Janie has to tell you!"

Play "show and tell" at home with things your child uses without your help. Let her call other adults and children on the telephone to tell about things that have happened or that she is looking forward to.

9

Activities to
Enhance Relating

It is often said that children develop in spite of our well-intentioned teaching. Often, all we really need to do is to provide ample chances for our children to explore on their own. Below is a laundry list of relationship-based activities to introduce to your son or daughter. Consider the list a springboard from which you can launch into your own ideas for enhancing your child's development. Take the ideas listed below and make them work for you, for your child, and for your family. While some ideas may seem simplistic and repetitive, they are perfect for most children. If your child wants to do the same thing over and over, that is perfectly normal and should be encouraged. If your child turns away, struggles, resists, or otherwise indicates she doesn't want to participate, listen to her. Children are notorious for disliking something once, then adoring it the next time, so don't give up—try, try again.

Play is "child's work" and your baby should spend much of her waking alert times in some sort of play. While the play activities listed below are organized into developmental categories, it is important to remember that play in one area develops all areas.

It is important to allow and encourage your child to explore her environment with as much independence and self-motivation as is safe for her age. As your child grows, her need for your supervision, direction, and motivation will vary. You might come to realize that your child resists your attempts to "teach" her. Listen to her. Allow her to explore and learn on her own. Provide the materials and the opportunity. While this independence is important, your child should never be completely unsupervised or allowed to use toys, tools, or appliances not intended for children her chronological or developmental age.

The most important principle in enhancing social development is experience. You must let your baby relate to a variety of people. Two-parent families that are small or families that consist of a single parent and a child have the biggest challenge in helping the child develop social relationships. These parents need to seek groups, invite visitors, or find other ways to introduce the child to a variety of people on a frequent basis. All experiences will not and should not be harmonious. It is very important that your child learn to resolve conflict, frustration, anger, fear, and shyness. From the earliest stages in infancy, watch your child's personality grow and her moods and emotions develop. Let her see your moods and how you handle them. As she becomes a toddler, she will want to be with other children. You may want to join a play group or preschool center to provide group interaction experiences for your toddler. Your role is to provide a socially diverse, rich, stimulating environment for her to explore relationships. Infants and toddlers who have had experiences with others enter school with developing social skills and a good social base.

The activities below link directly to the items in the checklist. If your child has scored low on a particular relating behavior that you think she should be able to do, study the activities in the list below and incorporate it into your child's routine. Feel free to adapt or expand the activity to suit your home and situation. Most of all, have fun with these activities, and encourage your child to be happy and friendly! Although they are designed to practice and reinforce specific aspects of relationships, they can not be successful until they're brought to life. Only you can make the learning process fun.

0-4 Months

Showing Excitement

When your baby wakes up from a nap, turn on the light and talk to her in a pleasant voice. Watch her reaction. She should show excitement by stiffening her body and legs, quieting, or flailing her arms. Her excitement should be unmistakable to you.

Show your own excitement at your baby's developmental achievements and her efforts by smiling and commenting to her about her actions.

Make time to tell others about your baby's achievements while she is present. She will sense your excitement.

Getting Attention

When your baby is content and alert, be present in the room, but not directly in front of her. Make normal sounds as you move about the room, and notice whether she makes different sounds or moves to get your attention. When she does, go to her and return her attention by talking to her or picking her up. Note whether, after you give her attention, she repeats the movement or sound.

Mirror Interest

Hold or lay your baby directly in front of a mirror. See if she shows interest in her mirror image by reaching toward the mirror, smiling, staring, or suddenly quieting. Talk to her, say her name, and move her hands and arms to attract her attention to her image.

Bring your baby to the mirror with you when you comb your hair or brush your teeth. Let her watch you and herself in the mirror.

Hand-Play

Watch your baby when she is content and alert in an infant seat. Watch to see if she begins to play with her own hands. See if she brings them together so that one hand touches or grabs the other as she watches them.

Play with your baby's hands. Move them in gentle, "patty cake"-like games. Gently move her hands up to her face and touch it. Let her see her hands as you move them.

Smiling and Laughing

Talk to your baby in a fun and pleasant voice and watch her reaction. Look to see if she smiles and laughs when you are talking to her. Her happy reaction shows that she is aware of you and likes your attention—the start of an important relationship. Smile and laugh when your baby "talks" to you. Let your baby see others smiling and hear people laughing.

5-8 Months

Baby Games

Spend at least 30 minutes to 1 hour each day specifically playing with your baby. Play baby games with your baby when she is content and alert. Games like "peek-a-boo," "this little piggy," "so big," and "where's the baby?" are great. Watch to see if she shows enjoyment by smiling and laughing.

Family Bonding

Let visitors hold your baby. Note her reaction to strangers. You should expect that she is more content and happier when held by familiar family members. This is a healthy distinction between relationships.

Hold your baby when she wants to be held, especially while in the company of those she does not know.

Early Separation

Parents should hand their baby over to baby-sitters or other family members from time to time. If your baby cries and fusses when separated, it indicates a normal developmental step at this age in her bonding with you.

Do not discourage your baby's cries when you leave her. Tell her you will be back and that you love her, then leave quickly and return when you say you will. Do this whenever you leave your baby's range of vision.

When you return, even if it is only from the next room, go to your baby, pick her up, cuddle her, and tell her something like "See, I came back just like I said I would."

Be consistent in your leaving routine. Always leave the same way calmly. Hold her while you talk with the caregiver, include her in the conversation, ask her for a kiss and give her one, tell her when you will be back, hug her before handing her into the arms of the caregiver, say good-bye, then leave quickly and directly. If your routine includes a wave from the window or door, do it once and go.

Acknowledge your baby's fear of strangers and of being left. Cuddle her while you tell her you know she is afraid but that it is okay and that you will be back. Keep it brief and convey your confidence in the caregiver.

Mirror Love

Seat your baby directly in front of a mirror. Now you should notice that she smiles and wants to touch her image and even "kiss" herself in the mirror.

Play with your baby in the mirror. Play baby games in front of the mirror. Place a safe mirror against a wall at floor level so your baby can see her own face.

Likes and Dislikes

Try giving your baby different toys or different foods from time to time. You should expect to see her letting you know clearly what she likes and doesn't like. With items she likes, you will see her smile, coo, or laugh, while with things she doesn't want anything to do with, she will cry, turn her head, stiffen, or kick. Acknowledge her likes and dislikes by saying things like "Janie doesn't like crackers? Okay, I know you don't like your medicine, but you must take it."

9-12 Months

Showing Moods

Watch your baby and note whether she expresses her moods and feelings. By now, it should be clear to you when she is happy, sad, mad, frustrated, excited, and puzzled.

Each time your baby shows a facial expression, name it for her. Say something like, "You look angry, but you may not play with the scissors," or "You look happy, do you like pictures of babies?" Do not try to change her moods, but acknowledge them.

Playing with Others

Encourage other adults and older children to play with your baby. She should enjoy playing with toys on the floor, dancing to music, dropping toys for "pickup," and playing "peek-a-boo" with others.

When your baby comes to you with a toy, play with her and the toy. Encourage her to tickle you by saying something like "It tickles when you touch ," then laugh and pretend to shy away. Tickle her back.

More Baby Games

Engage your baby in active baby games. Play "pat-a-cake," "peek-a-boo," and "so-big." During these games, your baby actively takes part and imitates you. Encourage other family members to play these games with her too. Make up your own games which use a repeated phrase or song and motions you can help your baby make.

Offering Toys

Sit with your baby on the floor with toys scattered within reach. Quietly play with the toys, and observe whether she offers, but may not actually let go of, the toys. This is a first step toward the concept of sharing toys.

Ask your baby if you can see the toys she is holding. Praise her when she shows them to you. When she is good at that, ask her to give them to you. Praise her when she does so, even if she does not let go.

Seeking Approval

When your baby does something wrong, say "no" in a clear, firm voice, letting her know of your disapproval. Note whether she immediately stops the behavior and shows some upset at making you unhappy. By responding to "no," she is showing that she wants your approval.

Show your baby approval for appropriate behavior. Say things like, "You are so smart to play with your toys that way," or "Is my baby sad?" or "Good for you, you let go of the plant" or "Look at you trying to walk." Touch her, pat her, stroke her, and kiss and hug her to show you approve of her behavior. Firmly tell your baby "no" and move her away from things she should not have or do, and interest her in other appropriate things. After a few times of hearing "no," your baby has probably learned what the word means because she will cry, move away, stop, or hurry and do as much as she can before you stop her. Don't worry if she doesn't stop—she still knows what the word means.

13-16 Months

Showing Affection

When you hold your baby, note whether she smiles and makes the effort to hug, kiss, or snuggle with you. At this age, she should actively seek and show affection.

Show your baby lots and lots of affection. All during her waking hours, smile at, kiss, hug, tickle, pat, hold, rock, and stroke her, and she will do the same to you and others.

Demonstrate appropriate affection to others in front of your baby and show her how to show affection for special toys.

Beginning to Share

Sit on the floor with your baby, toys scattered within reach. See if she will give you a toy and not want it back immediately. She may change her mind and see if you will give it back, so play along. But, most importantly, she will give you a toy without wanting it back immediately.

Play at taking and giving toys back to your baby. Start by taking them and then giving them right back. Ask your baby to give you a specific toy, repeating something like "Give it to me." Then gently take it away, keep it in her sight, and give it right back. If you must take away something that is unsafe, tell her that it is "not for babies." If you need to take something in order to fix it, let her come along and watch while you explain what you are doing and, if possible, give it right back.

Liking Children

It is important to give your baby the chance to be with other babies. You can start or join a play group or early childhood program that provides these opportunities. Watch from a distance and see if she enjoys being around other children. She should get excited and appear more content around them.

Frequently (two to three times a week) bring your baby to places where there are other children. Parks, libraries, playgrounds, stores, malls, and the homes of neighbors and friends with young children are good places to go. Allow your child to watch other children playing, and encourage her to play nearby. Fears should be acknowledged. Hold your baby if she wants to be held. Let her stay as near to you as she likes.

Chase Me, Catch Me

Play "I'm gonna get you." Exclaim "I'm gonna get you," then crawl toward your baby and tickle her with your chin. Encourage her to try to get away from you by saying something like "run, run." Then let her "get you."

Shows Many Emotions

Now your baby should show emotions beyond happiness, sadness, anger, and frustration—she may show excitement, joy, apprehension, anxiety, delight, and puzzlement. Name, acknowledge, and reinforce these emotions as your baby expresses them.

Show and name your own emotions when your baby is near. Guess at what she might be feeling using the events that have happened along with her facial and body reactions. When she flails her arms and bounces in anticipation, tell her she's excited. When she leans away from those she doesn't know, tell her she is scared or uncomfortable. When she furrows her brow while looking for something, tell her she is confused or puzzled.

17-20 Months

Demanding Company

When it is playtime, see if your toddler will play alone nearby. If she insists that you or another family member play with her, go ahead and play with her for a short while. Understand that this is a normal stage of development that shows she is seeking the company of others.

Start by keeping your toddler where the "action" is. Seat her where she can see what others are doing. Bring her close so that she can see. Give her a sample of what they are doing if it is safe to do so. Respond to your toddler's calls from her bed to be with others by getting her up or telling her something like "I know you want to be downstairs with us, but it is time for toddlers to go to sleep." When your toddler calls for you or others, go to her or call to her and let her join the activities. When your toddler strains to be part of the activity, acknowledge her wishes and bring her closer to the group.

Rough-Housing

When playing with your toddler, do a little rough-housing with her, as long as safety precautions are taken. She will enjoy wrestling, tickling, or being tossed about gently, and will ask for more.

Spend a little time each day rolling your baby enthusiastically around on the floor, tickling her energetically, lifting her swiftly into the air, and holding her above your head safely. Let her run to you, catch her, and swing her gently into the air. Let her lie on your shins while you lay on your back with knees bent, and gently bend and straighten your knees. While holding your baby on your hip, spin in a gentle circle. Let your baby run and tackle you while you sit, then fall back as she makes contact. Start out very gently and for just a little time, and increase the time and intensity a little bit every day for a few days, always being careful not to shake or jar your toddler.

Mirror Self-Image

In your toddler's room, be sure to place a mirror above a table or desk at the toddler's eye level, so that it's easy for her to look at her image. A safely positioned full-length mirror placed in the toddler's room at her height is also a good idea. Looking at her image helps her establish her self-concept. Don't be surprised if she spends a few minutes just looking at herself or talking to her image.

Provide your baby with a safe mirror placed at her level. At first, spend time playing with her in her mirror, making faces, looking in mouths, moving around, etc.

After face-washing, teeth-brushing, and dressing, tell her to go check herself in her mirror to make sure she is ready.

Helping Others

Be sure to let your toddler help you with household chores. She will want to help you, even though it may be more work for you. Her offers to help should be enthusiastically accepted and encouraged by everyone in the household. Give her additional opportunities by asking her to help with certain tasks, like dusting or using toddler-sized tools.

Keep your toddler with you while you work around the house. Encourage her efforts to help you by saying things like "You are trying to bring me the sandpaper. Thank you, you are such a good helper."

Showing Off

You will begin to notice your toddler showing off in various ways to get attention. She may play shy, act silly, be aggressive, or find other ways to be the center of attention. It's permissible to allow a certain amount of this behavior since it's an important step in learning to relate to others and building self-esteem. If your toddler does not show off, you can give her the chance to be the center of attention. For example, encourage her to sing a song or perform a dance, then applaud and tell her how wonderful she is.

Expose your toddler to other adults and children. Allow her to be "shy," silly and show off, but do not encourage her by drawing attention to her behavior. Talk about your toddler's behavior with her. Say things like "When you see other children, you sure act silly" or "Did you act silly so that those children would notice you?"

21-24 Months

Self-Talk

While your toddler is playing, you may notice her talking to herself or to her toys. This is a normal stage in development, so let her play. She may even carry on long conversations with herself or her toys. To encourage this behavior in a toddler who doesn't talk to herself, sit alongside your toddler when she playing with toys on the floor. Play by yourself so she can watch you, and talk to yourself and to the toys. Using any toy, move it around and talk to yourself about what you are doing with it, what you will do with it, or talk as if you were the toy. Say things like "I'm going to run over all the blocks and crash into the toy box and you will never find me, ha ha." Watch to see if your toddler starts to talk to herself.

Parallel Play

When your toddler is in a room with other children, you may notice that she prefers to play alone in the room, rather than interact with the other children. This is known as parallel play and is perfectly normal at this age. Being comfortable in the company of others is a step toward learning to relate to others. Be sure to give your toddler opportunities to be with other children by starting or joining play groups or special infant and preschool programs that bring children together in a positive way.

Expose your toddler to other children. Form a play group with friends, play outside in a neighborhood with other children, join your local preschool PTA and bring your toddler to the child care set up during meetings, go to the park and playground, or go to fast food restaurants with play areas. At first she may just watch, but likely she will soon begin to play at least by herself, then follow along and finally play with other children.

Sharing Attention

When you are busy on the telephone or talking with someone else and your toddler comes and "tugs" on you, makes a fuss, and wants your attention (and it's not an emergency), tell her clearly *once* that you are busy and that she must wait a few minutes. Then ignore her pleas until you are ready (a few minutes, or whatever you promised). Start by expecting your toddler to wait 30 seconds to 1 minute, then gradually extend the time by adding a minute or so each time.

When you have company, alternate your attention from the company to your toddler. Delay responding to your toddlers demands if you are engaged with another person. Pick her up, hug her, or hold her hands while you continue to pay attention to another. After a brief time, announce "Now it's your turn," and respond to your toddler. Your physical touch reminds her that you love her and you know she is there but that she must wait.

Pleasing Others

You should notice your toddler looking for ways to please you and others. Make sure she notices when you try to please others. For example, when someone is sick, you make them feel better; when someone drops something, you pick it up for them; when someone is sad, you try to make them happy, and so forth.

Clearly express to your toddler when you are pleased with her behavior. Your facial expression, your words, and your actions should all convey the same pleased message. Say things like "I really like when you use your words," and then hug her. Also express clearly your expectations for her behavior and tell her in words and actions what is not acceptable behavior. Say things like "You may not bite —that is not acceptable behavior" and remove her from the area, showing your displeasure at her behavior. This is a good time to start telling her that it is her behavior that is not good, but that you still love her.

Ordering Others

You may notice your toddler giving orders to other children or family members. She may sound "bossy" as she hollers at or commands people to do what she wants. This is normal, and she will soon discover how tolerant other people will be. She may be commanding toward the dog and her toys, too.

Play with your toddler, letting her be the boss. Have her tell you and show you what she wants you to do. Try not to suggest anything, but let her be the director of your play. You will be amazed at her ideas and directions and will appreciate another aspect of childhood.

25-30 Months

Miniature Mom and Dad

It may really surprise you when you see your toddler imitating some of your actions. For example, she may put her hands on her waist, shake her head, and tell the dog to "go to bed this very minute." She may copy your mannerisms, the way you hold your head, point your finger, and the tone of your voice. This imitation is normal. You will want to be careful about the words and gestures you use—you may soon find your toddler doing and saying things you don't want her to imitate.

Give your toddler plenty of toys that let her pretend to be an adult or older child—safe kitchen utensils, child-size cars, toy phones, toy computers, and lawn mowers—all the things she sees you use. Let her watch you and be around you doing the things you do, and soon she will be imitating you.

Making Friends

Be sure to give your toddler opportunities to be among children, of all ages. Attend play groups, visit other families, or visit playgrounds where other children play. Encourage your toddler to approach other children and let them approach her. She may show affection for a particular toddler, usually of the opposite sex, at this age. She may kiss him, hug him, and just want to follow him and be with him.

Show affection for others in front of your toddler. This is how she will begin to learn about appropriate displays of affection for others. When she shows affection appropriately, encourage her by saying things like "I like the way you show Joseph that you like him." Encourage attachment to your toddler's choice of a friend by making time for them to be together.

Testing "No"

Continue to follow through on rules with your toddler. Consistency is crucial. For example, when you are washing your toddler's face, she may say "no." It's important to realize that she is testing your reaction. You must be firm and let her know in no uncertain terms that she is NOT to say "no" to you. Then proceed with washing her face.

Respond to your toddler's "no" by acknowledging it calmly and easily. Resist explaining your action in great detail. When your toddler gets to choose, avoid letting her waver back and forth between yes and no. Stick firm to most decisions with clear resolve so that your toddler learns to read your verbal and physical messages.

Relating Feelings

Your toddler should now be able to better communicate her feelings to you. She should be using both words and gestures to show how she feels. When she is expressing an emotion to you, reinforce it by saying, "Why are you crying and sitting in the corner? Are you sad? What is making you sad?"

Take the time to calmly listen and watch your toddler express her feelings. When she is through, say something like "Your stamping and hollering tell me that you are very angry, what should we do?"

Using Names

Your toddler should now be attaching relationship names to members of the household. She should be using names like "Daddy," "Baby," "Mommy," and "Grandma," showing that she is becoming aware of the relationships in the family. If she isn't using these terms, be sure to reinforce them by saying, "Where's Daddy?" Let her point to Daddy, and then say, "Who's that?"

Expose your toddler to others she does not know. Acknowledge your toddler's accurate description of children and adults by saying things like "Yes, that is a woman like Mommy" or "Yes, that child is someone's baby" or "Yes, that man is like Daddy."

31-36 Months

Playing Cooperatively

Give your toddler the opportunity to be with groups of children, or at least with one or two other children. When they are playing with toys or playing on the playground, you should notice your toddler playing cooperatively with another toddler. She should seek out the playmate, share the toys and the activity, and talk with her. If she would rather play alone, be sure to provide more opportunities for her to play in the company of others. Participate in play groups, or enroll her in a part time preschool program, and visit her as she plays with the other children. When she is with another toddler, you can promote cooperation by encouraging her to share her toys, or to show something to the other toddler.

Invite another preschooler to play with your child. At first, have them play in an area near you. When you see appropriate interactive play, say something like "Look at you two building, you do a great job together." Continue to comment on cooperative play, avoiding remarks about conflicts. Once these are worked out, say something like "It is so much fun to work things out so that you can keep playing." Keep first play sessions short, separating preschoolers to different activities. Extend cooperative play time as the preschoolers learn to work things out.

Pretending

Observe your toddler during playtime. You should see her pretending to be doing things that she sees you and others do. For example, she may pretend to make the coffee, polish her shoes, read a book, or write a letter. Play along with her and encourage her game of pretending. She may also pretend to be a character from a story or a video.

Demonstrate pretend play to your preschooler by telling her you are going to pretend to be someone you both know fairly well. Pretend that you are that person, doing the things he or she does. Read a story to your preschooler and suggest that you both pretend to be characters in the story—"I'll be the bear and you can be the kitty."

Showing Disgust

Your toddler should now be forming opinions about things in her world, and a key opinion to show at this age is disgust. She may begin by mimicking you showing disgust at certain smells, sights, and objects. Then she may even get dramatic by holding her nose, and "going on" about how disgusting something is. Reinforce her opinion by sharing your own, like "Whew, you're right, that really does smell just awful!"

Show your disgust at smells, pictures, objects, and behaviors. Shake your head, grimace, turn away, and say things like "That's disgusting," or "Ick, that's awful" or "Get that out of here, it's disgusting." Briefly tell your preschooler why it is disgusting by saying, "I can't stand that smell" or "It makes me feel sick to see that" or "You know that behavior is unacceptable."

Watching TV

Provide your toddler with the opportunity to watch some of the better children's programming on television and on videos. Monitor the time spent in front of the TV, so it is not excessive (an hour throughout the day is more than ample). She may show interest by attentively watching certain TV programs, commercials, or special videos.

Supervised, limited TV viewing can introduce your preschooler to things she may not otherwise be able to see or hear. Her interest in new and different things can be measured in part by her interest in TV. Use TV to talk about things your preschooler sees. Ask her questions, encourage her questions, and comment on the things you see on TV and their connection to your family life, morals, and values.

Playing in a Group

Be sure to give your toddler the chance to be in a play group with other children. Observe the group and note whether your toddler behaves like a member of the group, rather than associating with just one other toddler. She should be taking turns and helping other group members.

Meet with a play group of about four children and let them play. Refrain from directing or organizing the activity, instead, let the children decide what it is they will do. Later, suggest a game that requires the preschoolers to take turns, then to cooperate in order to reach an objective.

37-42 Months

Seeking Attention and Praise

Watch to see if your preschooler shows pride in her accomplishments. She should be calling attention to her own performance. For example, your preschooler may say, "Look at me, look at me" or "I made this" or "Watch what I can do," to get your attention. She may be incessant at seeking this attention when there are visitors present. Give her the attention she seeks and praise her accomplishments at appropriate moments. This is important to her growing self image and self-confidence.

Pay attention to your preschooler's accomplishments. Say things like "good job." Soon she will be calling attention to her performance. Continue to praise her efforts. Ask to see the things she has done and ask about what she is planning to do.

Interacting with Others

Give your preschooler the chance to be around other children on a regular basis (several times a week). Watch to see if she interacts with them beyond playing. She should be talking with them, sharing ideas and experiences, and showing things to others. If she is not interacting, you may want to start out letting her play with one or two other children, then gradually expand the experiences to larger groups.

Let your child play with children who are at a higher level of development in relating to others. Sometimes these will be older children. This will expose her to children who interact beyond playing. Look for children who plan their play together ("You be the dog, and I'll be the dad, then you will bark and I'll pretend to take you to the park."). Encourage your preschooler to show her toys to others, tell what she did or what she is going to do, and talk about her ideas for play.

Showing Sympathy

Your preschooler's emotions should be expanding beyond herself to showing feelings for others—in particular, sympathy. Your preschooler should be asking questions like "Are you okay?" or "Oh no, that must hurt" to show genuine concern for someone else. She should also offer help and gestures of comfort. If she is not showing sympathy, model it for her. Let her see you show sympathy for someone else. For example, say, "Oh no, Janie, look. Mario, hurt his knee." Then go to Mario with Janie watching, and say, "Oh Mario, you hurt your knee. I bet that hurts, doesn't it? Let me give you a hug so you'll feel better. Should we put a bandage on it?" and so forth.

Show genuine concern for your preschooler when she comes to you for attention. If you feel she is faking an injury, say something like "It doesn't seem so bad to me, but I bet it hurts you. You must need some loving up." When your preschooler shows concern for others, encourage her by telling her with your words and gestures that you like how she shows she cares.

Having Favorite Activities

As your preschooler is expressing more and more opinions and personal choices, you should find that she clearly has favorite activities. She should be spending 20 minutes or more of uninterrupted time doing activities like playing with sand, building blocks, dolls, and trucks, or blowing bubbles. Be sure to provide opportunities for a variety of activities, so she can start showing preferences.

Let your preschooler suggest her own activities and time how long she plays without loosing interest. As she loses interest, suggest a simple idea for her to try to extend her interest. Keep your preschooler supplied with all kinds of arts and crafts materials by saving odds and ends around the house. Avoid specific projects that match a model made by someone more developed than your preschooler.

Being Friendly

It's important for you as a parent to model friendly behavior. It is natural at this age that your preschooler is a happy little tyke. She should be showing remarkable cooperation and a cheerful disposition most of the time. If she isn't, it is usually a reflection of the moods and attitudes of those around her. When you are happy and smiling, show a sense of humor, and are flexible and loving, your preschooler will be too.

Encourage your preschooler's expression of happiness by saying things like "You are very happy, did you sleep well?" or "I really like when you wake up happy." Encourage your preschooler to greet others who greet her. Explain that when someone you know and like and feel safe with talks to you, you talk back to them to show that you hear them.

43-48 Months

Sharing Toys

Provide opportunities for your preschooler to play with children in a group, not necessarily just at the park, but in a group where children have toys and objects to explore. Watch your preschooler to see if she is sharing. She should be very willing to share toys, even at home, feeling confident that she will get them back.

Allow your preschooler to have a few special toys she never has to share. Teach her to explain about her "special toy" to others who want it. Avoid speaking for your preschooler. Have her find some toys she is willing to share and show them to others. It will help her if she is able to say to others something like "Here, play with these, but you must leave them at my house." Praise her when she shares toys even for a very brief time.

Take opportunities to point out when you share with her, when others share, and what happens when she does and doesn't share. Say things like "I will share my cookie with you. What will you share with me?" or "Thomas gave you his toy, he does great sharing" or "Thank you for sharing your candy with me, I'll share my pop with you." Strike sharing deals with your preschooler, like "I am willing to buy one popcorn and one drink if you are willing to share with Michael." If she is not willing to share, give it all to the child who will share or one item to each child, or do not buy it. Use simple phrases to comment on how sharing makes all of us happy, like "When we share, we all have fun," or "When you share your cars with John, John shares his train with you."

Showing Self-Control

As your preschooler matures, you will notice occasions when previously she would have thrown a tantrum, or touched something she shouldn't have, or would otherwise have been impulsive without showing self-control. Now, you should be seeing signs of self-control. You should see her resist the temptation to handle forbidden objects, hit someone, or say "no" to you.

When you see this, you can reinforce it by saying things like "That's a big girl. I like the way you didn't get mad about that," and eventually simply accept it as natural, and not make a big deal out of it.

Establish clear standards and expectations for behavior, like "You must talk in a normal, happy voice or we will leave" or "We are going to the store to buy groceries, we will not be spending our money on candy," or "these things are for looking at, you may not touch them."

Plan a few trips or experiences to demonstrate your resolve in your expectations of your preschooler's behavior. Actually plan to follow through on your consequences—leave the store immediately, stop the activity and put away the materials, send your preschooler to her room, separate her from the group. Develop a signal or warning system. Allow one or two reminders, then be ready to follow through with natural consequences meaningful to your preschooler.

Participating in a Group

By now, your preschooler should be involved in some sort of preschool or play group that meets at least twice a week. Observe your preschooler as she interacts naturally in the group. Also talk with the teacher or group leader and ask about your preschooler's involvement. At this age, she should be actively and appropriately participating in whole group activities that are led by a teacher or supervisor.

Take turns leading or supervising a small play group of four or five children. Expect appropriate behavior from all the preschoolers.

Enroll your child in your local library's preschool story time. Request or organize a library story time that your preschooler can attend.

Having a Best Friend

If your preschooler has been participating in group activities or is in contact with other children at home or in the neighborhood, she is probably attached to one friend more than any other. Your preschooler's primary friend at this age will most likely be of the same sex. If your preschooler does not have a best friend, perhaps she hasn't had the opportunity. Since it's an important stage in developing relationships, enrolling your preschooler in some sort of play group or preschool program is a good avenue for enhancing socialization.

Encourage a special friend by arranging times for the preschoolers to play with each other. Be sure the friend is your child's choice.

Respecting Property

Let your preschooler handle or touch your belongings with care. She should now show respect and handle them carefully, realizing that they are important to you. Watch her about the household to see if she continues respecting others and their things.

Start by expecting your preschooler to take care of her toys. Toys she does not take care of, or breaks during tantrums or in anger, should be taken away. Require your child to help fix and clean up even accidental breakage or damage. Another natural consequence of breaking something is for a preschooler to give up a favored toy to replace a broken or damaged one. Take away toys treated inappropriately, saying something like "You treat this so roughly, you must not like it, so I will take it away." Keep toys sorted and on shelves, storing those you do not have room for, and occasionally switching with those that are being used.

49-60 Months

Making Friends

Give your preschooler the chance to regularly interact with groups of children, and you will notice that she now chooses friends of the same sex. Girls prefer girls as friends, and boys prefer boys. This is a normal stage in the process of developing relationships. She should, however, have access and opportunity to play with children of both sexes.

Expose your child her to larger, mixed groups of children. Ask her about her friends and what she does and what she likes.

Performing for Others

Allow your preschooler the opportunity to put on a performance or show for you and others. She may want to turn a somersault, sing a song, or dance in front of a group while greatly enjoying the attention and recognition. Praise her performance and encourage her to put on these little acts that are important for her self-confidence and self-esteem.

Provide your child with finger-puppets, hand-puppets, and dress-up clothing. Show her how to tell a story with puppets, action figures, dolls, and stuffed animals. Take turns with your child putting on plays or shows. Let your child plan a play or show and direct you in what to do and say. Make puppets with old socks or paper bags, glue, and scraps of things from around the house and yard.

Having Secrets

Whisper a secret to your preschooler. Whisper it in her ear so no one else can hear, and let her enjoy the secrecy. Tell her that she must keep it a secret and tell no one. When she does keep the secret, praise her for doing so. Let her tell her own secrets, and enjoy sharing and keeping them.

Play "telephone" by whispering a word or short phrase to her and have her whisper it to another with the last person announcing what was heard.

Responding to Praise and Blame

When your preschooler accomplishes something or does something that pleases you, praise her, and watch her reaction. She should "shine" in the attention for her accomplishment. When she does something wrong, hold her responsible and be clear that you are not pleased with what she did. Once again watch her reaction—your disappointment should make her feel "bad," and she may cry because you are not happy with her because of what she did.

Talk about how you feel when your child tells you "thank you" or "I love you" or "I like how you did that." After praising your child, ask her how it feels. Does she like that feeling? Next time your child gets in trouble, ask her how it feels to be punished. Draw your child's attention to her feelings when she is called names, left out of a game, or yelled at by another. Talk about incidents she observes and ask her how she feels when similar things happen to her. Share how you would feel if it were you.

Preferring to be with Children

Let your preschooler be present in company that includes both children and adults. At this age, she will seek out the company of the children over the company of the adults, showing that she is relating to children of her own age.

Require adult time for yourself to do adult things while your child does children's things. Explain clearly that you expect her to leave you alone. Put her in the safe company of other children during your adult time. Respond to her desire to be with other children by letting her invite others over, going to parks and playgrounds with supervision, or playing outside near home.

61-72 Months

Behaving in Public

Provide chances for your child to eat in public, go shopping, and attend other events. Teach her common rules of etiquette such as when to say "please," "thank you, " "excuse me, " and "pleased to meet you," without prompting. When she does act polite and show socially acceptable behavior, praise her.

Use good manners in your everyday life so that your child learns by example. Say "please" and "thank you" in dealing with your family members, your child, and other children. Open doors for others, let others pass in front, help others, and smile and say kind things. Explain briefly why you do those things—how it makes you feel good to help others; how others are happier to help you when you say "please" and "thank you." Have tea parties, play restaurant, pretend to be on trips, and practice using good manners. Reward your child by taking her "out" specifically to show off her good manners and helpful behavior.

Following Rules

Your child will have an easier time understanding and following rules at school if she has had to learn and follow rules at home. When she breaks a rule, like not putting her toys away, remind her about the rules and follow through with a natural consequence like "no playing until the toys are picked up."

Learn the classroom or play group rules and ask your child about them. When she talks about her experiences and those of her classmates, ask about the rules and what happens when they are broken.

Playing Competitively

Let your child compete in play group and school races and contests. At this stage, racing, comparing performances with others, and winning become very important. But it's also important that she experience losing and learn to accept it graciously.

Let your child develop her own views of competition through experience. Her announcements about winning and losing should be acknowledged and talked about. Talk freely about races and competitions she is a part of, or that others are talking about. Experiencing competition is a way of learning about the world and other people.

Initiating

Encourage your child to take the initiative to introduce herself to others. When visiting a park or playground, encourage her to say "hello" to other children, to ask them to play, and to show them things.

Play "How do you do?" by pretending with your child that you are meeting for the first time or seeing each other at school or elsewhere. Walk around, then "see" each other, shake hands, and say "How do you do?" or "How are you?" or "Hello." Take turns with your child pretending that you are the teachers, principal, children, parents, helpers, or custodians. The next time it happens for real, wink at your child or otherwise subtly remind her of your practice.

Understanding Fairness

When you punish your child for doing something wrong, be sure the punishment is fair and is a logical consequence of the behavior. For example, if she tracks mud into the kitchen, fair punishment would be cleaning her shoes and wiping up the mud. At this age, she should accept fair play and fair punishment, and not protest.

Refuse to play games with your child when she intentionally breaks rules. Comment when your child breaks rules, so that she realizes that you know. Express your feelings about playing with someone who breaks the rules. Explain why you like to play games. Show her examples of fair play and enforce consequences of unfair play, like being removed from the game.

10

Activities to Enhance Thinking

It is often said that children develop in spite of our well-intentioned teaching. Often, all we really need to do is to provide ample chances for our children to explore on their own. Below is a laundry list of thinking activities to introduce to your son or daughter. Consider the list a springboard from which you can launch into your own ideas for enhancing your child's development. Take the ideas listed below and make them work for you, for your child, and for your family. While some ideas may seem simplistic and repetitive, they are perfect for most children. If your child wants to do the same thing over and over, that is perfectly normal and should be encouraged. If your child turns away, struggles, resists, or otherwise indicates she doesn't want to participate, listen to her. Children are notorious for disliking something once, then adoring it the next time, so don't give up—try, try again.

Play is "child's work" and your baby should spend much of her waking alert times in some sort of play. While the play activities listed below are organized into developmental categories, it is important to remember that play in one area develops all areas.

It is important to allow and encourage your child to explore her environment with as much independence and self-motivation as is safe for her age. As your child grows, her need for your supervision, direction, and motivation will vary. You might come to realize that your child resists your attempts to "teach" her. Listen to her. Allow her to explore and learn on her own. Provide the materials and the opportunity. While this independence is important, your child

should never be completely unsupervised or allowed to use toys, tools or appliances not intended for children her chronological or developmental age.

Development of intellect, more than any other area, is reflected in progress in all other areas. Given the opportunity to use all of her senses to explore her environment and talk about her experiences in a loving, accepting family, your child's thinking skills will blossom. The most important principle in enhancing mental development is experience. You must let your baby explore her environment. Parents who solve problems for their children, or do not let them make mistakes, are impeding their children's growth and development. From the earliest stages in infancy, place your child on a blanket on the floor or in a "playpen." Let her move, play with objects, and go exploring. As she becomes a toddler, she will wear you out with her constant adventures and questions. Your role is to provide a safe, supervised environment for her to explore, and then let her go! Infants and toddlers who are allowed to be active problem-solvers and question-askers enter school eager to learn.

The activities below link directly to the items in the checklist. If your child has scored low on a particular thinking behavior that you think she should be able to do, study the activity in the list below and incorporate it into your child's routine. Feel free to adapt or expand the activity to suit your home and situation. Most of all, have fun with these activities! Although they are designed to practice and reinforce specific movements, they cannot be successful until they're brought to life; only you can make the learning process fun.

0-4 Months

Eye-Tracking

When your baby is alert and content, hold a brightly colored toy 9 to 10 inches from her face and move it slowly in an arc from side to side. Watch to see if her eyes follow the toy. You can even capture her attention with your face (without talking), then move your face from side to side to see if she "watches" you.

Move toys in circles and in up-and-down and back-and-forth motions while your baby watches. Move toys slowly so that she can focus and follow them.

Play a "duck-and-peek" sort of game where you move your face into your baby's view from all sorts of directions and at different speeds.

Place your baby in a safe place where she can watch what you are doing. Household chores are interesting to her and will encourage her to watch and move her eyes and head.

Have company visit your home—young children are especially good visitors for your baby. The unusual sound of new voices will encourage your baby to turn her head toward their voices.

Exploring with Her Mouth

Give your baby a rattle to see if she brings it to her mouth. You will probably notice that she puts her fist into her mouth, and anything that's in her grasp will be brought to her mouth, where she "mouths" it in curiosity.

Put safe rattles in your baby's hand, gently shake her hand—then gently move the rattle, still in her hand to her mouth. Ask her if it tastes good!

Provide lots of "choke-proof" toys made from non-toxic materials. Let your child examine and "taste" them all. Laugh, clap, and smile when she does and talk about what she did.

Responding to Sound

In a quiet room, approach your baby when she is healthy, awake, and content. Stand to one side where she cannot see you, and make a sound without using your voice. Tap your foot, ring a little bell, crumple newspaper, and watch to see if she turns her head toward the sound. Try this from other positions in the room on other occasions. If your child does not respond, you must talk with your pediatrician.

Make sounds both loud and soft by clapping, singing, stomping, and clanging pans, and toys all around your baby to encourage her to turn her head toward the sound. Give her the toy or show her how you made the sound when she looks.

Keep your baby where the action is, so that she can listen to and discover the source of the ringing phone, the droning vacuum cleaner, the television, the radio, the conversations, the clang of cooking pans, the clink of forks and knives, the rush of running water, and, most importantly, voices in conversation. She will learn how smart she is when you show her where these sounds are coming from.

Whisper to your baby, telling her how much you love her, saying her name, and telling her the names of everyone who loves her. Talk in different voices and laugh and smile at her response.

Exploring Faces

Hold your baby so that your face is within her reach. Put her hand on your face and let her touch. Watch to see if she grabs at, pets, swipes, pokes, or pulls at your nose, eyes, hair, chin, or mouth. Watch to see if she explores the faces of other people too.

Encourage your baby to touch your face and the faces of family members and close friends by moving close to her own. Move her hands to your cheek, then kiss them, then make her pat your nose, then playfully "bite" or "mouth" her fingers.

Knowing the Family

When your baby is alert and comfortable in an infant seat, have family members and unfamiliar visitors talk to and visit with her. Watch to see if her reaction is different when approached by a familiar family member than it is with an unfamiliar visitor. If not, be sure family members hold her and play with her more often.

Introduce your baby to family members and close friends, by having them around her often and regularly. Say the name of each family member each time your baby looks at or otherwise responds to them. Encourage family members to play with your baby and use their own names. When you call out for another family member, encourage your baby to look for that person, then exclaim "Here is Tom!" when Tom arrives. Pay attention to your baby's response when you call for another family member. Tell her when she looks around how smart she is.

Ask your baby "Where is Mommy?" or "where is Daddy?" or "where is Michael?" etc., and tell her the answers by pointing at each person. If she looks around for the named person, tell her how wonderful she is.

5-8 Months

Looking for the Hidden Toy

Lay your baby on her stomach. Place a toy on the floor within her reach and let her reach for it and study it. Then place a blanket or towel over the toy in front of her. Watch to see if she looks for it. She may not find it, but she should look for it with her eyes and reach for it where she last saw it.

Hide toys while your baby watches. Play "peek-a-boo" with a toy. Play variations of "peek-a-boo" by hiding your face behind your hands, under a cloth, or behind or under objects.

Pulling a String for a Toy

Use a pull-toy or tie a piece of yarn or a cord safely to a toy. While your baby is watching, pull the toy so it comes to her. Then put the string in her hand and see if she pulls it to her.

Put the string of a toy in your baby's hand, then move her hand and arm back or up and down while she watches the toy move around.

Holding More Than One Toy

When your baby is sitting safely propped, put a toy in one of her hands. Then hold another toy directly in front of her. Watch to see if she keeps holding on to one while she reaches for the other. When your child doesn't drop one toy in order to get another, she recognizes that she can hold on to one and reach for another one.

Encourage your baby to hold more than one toy by placing toys in her hand. Laugh and smile and encourage her by saying things like "Look at you, you have two toys."

Encourage your baby to reach for more toys by offering her another while she holds one.

Exploring Toys

Shake toys while your baby watches, then give it to her. Praise her exploration by asking "What does that taste like?" or "Do you like that sound?"

Body-Exploring

When you are changing your baby or during bath time, encourage her to touch and grab her toes or her fingers. Let her pat, grab, suck, and just explore her own fists, toes, and fingers. Don't be concerned if your baby touches her genitalia; it is normal and a sign of healthy exploration as she learns about her own body.

Show your baby her feet. Gently hold her feet and tickle her stomach with her own feet. Hold your baby's feet and hands together and gently rock and roll her.

Slowly bicycle your baby's legs. Gently move your baby's arms in "cheer-leading" style. Move her hands together over her head, across her chest, and down to her sides.

9-12 Months

Holding Toys

When your baby is sitting up playing, hand her a toy. Then hand her another, and while she is holding those two, hand her a third toy. She should experiment and find a way to hold three small toys all at the same time. Help her only if she needs it.

Place small, safe toys around your baby. If she does not pick any up, offer her one, then another, and then another. If she drops one to take another, move her hands so that she can hold two in one hand and take another. No matter what she does, praise her and comment on what she has done. If she resists holding two toys in one hand, do not pressure her to perform.

Finding the Hidden Toy

During playtime, put a toy on the floor in front of your baby. Put a blanket or towel over the toy to hide it. She will know where it is. Watch her uncover the toy by pulling off the blanket. If she doesn't, let her watch you do it. Let her watch you put a toy in your hand, then close your fist, and let her point to the fist that has it.

Hide toys while your baby watches, and tell her how terrific it is when she looks for them.

Using Containers

Seat your baby on the floor with several toys and a container. You can use a box, a plastic bowl, a bucket, or a dump truck. Tell her, "Put the toys in the box." Then show her how to pick them up one at a time and put them in the box. Then watch to see if she does it, and if she does, say, "Good, Janie, that's right. Pick up the toys and put them in the box." If she doesn't, then put a toy in her hand and guide it to the box to drop it in.

Give your baby plastic bowls and cups to play with. Show her how to put things into bowls and cups, then shake and rattle the container. Tell her how smart she is when she puts things into dump trucks, wagons, boxes, etc.

Copying Actions

When your child is seated watching you, say, "Janie, pat-a-cake, pat-a-cake," then clap your hands and see if she copies you. Try other simple actions like ringing a bell, stirring a spoon, or shaking a rattle to see if she copies your actions.

Scribble, ring a bell, tap a spoon, or push a button while your baby watches. Gently move her hands and arms to do the same thing. Say something like "Ring the bell! Isn't that a pretty sound?" and repeat the same motions.

Busy Hands

Seat your child on the floor and give her a toy to hold in one hand. Then show her the other toys on the floor within her reach. Watch to see if she holds onto the first toy while exploring the other toys on the floor with her other hand.

Give your baby a toy to hold, then show her something new. If she drops the first toy, tuck it back into her hand or under her arm while she explores the new toy. Let your baby hold things with one hand while she feeds herself finger foods or holds a bottle.

13-16 Months

Simple Puzzles

Get a two- or five-piece simple puzzle for your baby. Wooden ones are the most durable for this age. Some puzzles have little knobs or handles on them for easy pick up and placement. When you have her attention, show her how to pick up one piece and try it in a couple of places, then fit it into the correct one. Talk her through it—for example, say, "Where does this piece go? In here? No, it doesn't fit. In here? No, it doesn't fit. In here? Yes, there it fits!" Then let her try to fit a piece. When she succeeds, clap your hands and get excited over her accomplishment.

Make your own shape puzzles out of corrugated cardboard or foam rubber. Be sure the puzzle pieces are no smaller than your child's hand. Let your baby play with the puzzle pieces, then show her how to put a round piece into its place. Gently move her hand to place the piece.

Turning Things Right-Side-Up

Place some toys in front of your baby upside-down, and some right-side-up. First, watch to see if she turns the upside-down toys right-side-up. If she does, praise her by saying, "Yes, Janie. Turn it over. We don't want it upside-down." If she doesn't do it on her own, demonstrate. For example, point to an upside-down truck and say, "Oh no, this truck is upside-down. Let's fix it. Let's turn it over." Then let her help you with the next one.

Place some overturned toys in a row and move down the row turning them upright. Each time you come to a toy, say something like, "Oh-oh, upside-down," then turn it upright. Put toys away with right sides up so that your baby gets used to seeing them in an upright position.

Dumping Things Out

Give your baby a plastic bottle and some raisins or dry cereal pieces. Show her how to pick up one piece and drop it in the bottle. Then let her try. Guide her hand if you need to. After several pieces are in the bottle, tell her to take them out. Watch to see if she turns it over to dump them out. If she doesn't, then show her and have her repeat it with another bottle of objects to dump out.

Give your baby a cup or bowl to hold, put an object in it, then gently move her hand and arm to dump the object out. Demonstrate dumping things out of a cup.

Scribbling

Seat your baby in her high chair or on a booster chair at a table. Have ready some large, fat crayons and blank sheets of paper. Tell her to draw a picture on the paper. Then show her how to draw by making a line and a circle, or draw a little picture, using lines and circles. Turn the paper over to a clean side. Then put the crayon in her hand, guide it to the paper, and help her make her own mark. Watch to see if she goes ahead and scribbles on her own.

Pointing to Body Parts

During dressing or bathing, point to your baby's hands, arms, legs, nose, and other body parts and say, "Where is your nose?" Then point to it and touch it and say, "Here is your nose," and so forth. Then ask her if she can point to these body parts. Make it fun with hugging and tickling, and try to get her to repeat the name of each part.

Holding your baby on your lap, sing or chant "head, shoulders, knees and toes" while you gently move your baby's hands to touch her own body parts as they are named. Have your baby point to named body parts on a doll, on another person, or on herself. Gently move her hand to the correct body part or point to your own to help her. Don't avoid naming and identifying genitalia.

17-20 Months

Tool Playing

Play tools are a marvelous way for your toddler to practice different actions she sees you and others do with tools. It's a good idea for your toddler to have her own little hammer, saw, broom, lawn mower, phone, and stove, among other toy appliances and tools. When you are using a real hammer or other tool around the house, let her watch you. Talk to her and show her what you are doing and why. "This is a hammer. I need it to pound this nail in the wall." Let her bring her tools beside you so she can be your little helper.

Give your toddler a toy saw, hammer, steering wheel, fork, knife, spoon, or spatula and say something like "What do you do with a saw?" Show her what to do with each and let her watch people using real tools. Use simple two- or three-word phrases to describe the actions and tell her when she uses play tools correctly.

Imitating Housework

Be sure to let your toddler watch you and "help" you when you are doing household chores. Talk to her when you are doing things, saying things like

"Look, these are all clean. Now we have to fold them." Watch to see if, in her own pretend play, she imitates some of the chores she sees you do. Reinforce her imitation, and say things like "Wow, you are mowing the front yard. What a good helper you are!"

Let your toddler watch you do housework, then include housework materials in her play things. Give her a dust rag, a safe empty spray bottle, and a small broom to keep in her "house." Comment on her imitation by saying things like "You can dust just like I do" or "You are sweeping the floor with me."

Pointing to More Body Parts

When you are dressing your toddler, or are in front of a mirror with her, ask her to point to and name her tummy, foot, knee, hand, finger, ear, or eye. Help her if she gets stuck on any parts.

Practice pointing to body parts with your toddler using a doll. Say, "Where is the baby's tummy?" and so forth. Do the same with pictures of characters in books.

Point to any body part and ask your toddler, "Is this your nose?" If you are pointing to her nose, say yes with her. If you are not pointing to her nose, say no with her followed by "That is not your nose, where is your nose?" Repeat with as many body parts as you can think of. If you are uncomfortable naming private parts, use age-appropriate pictures.

Two-Piece Puzzles

Get at least one simple shape puzzle for your toddler. The best ones are durable and made of wood with little handles or knobs on the pieces of simple geometric shapes—circles, squares, and triangles. At this age, watch for her to be able to place two different pieces correctly. Show her how to put a piece in the right space. Make it a fun game.

Borrow simple shape puzzles from your library or swap puzzles with others. Work with your toddler naming and tracing the shapes and respective places for shapes with fingers, matching shapes and places for shapes, then finally placing shapes in the correct spot.

Using Chairs for Reaching

Have a sturdy step stool of some sort so that your toddler can climb up to reach things. When she is trying to get something that is beyond her reach, and can't, tell her to move the stool to where she needs it, then to stand on it. For example, if she can't reach the bathroom faucet, but wants a drink, show her how to move the stool to the cabinet, then stand on it, turn the faucet, and get her own drink. Next time, don't show her, but tell her instead, and watch to see if she does it on her own.

Place things your toddler wants out of reach. When she asks for those things, tell her yes she can have them, then ask her how she can get them. Pause, then say something like "Go get your stool, stand on it, and see if you can reach it." Once successful at that, move the things a little farther away and when the stool doesn't reach, wait to see if she solves the problem herself. If she doesn't, ask what she might do to get the object. Try your best not to give her clues and ideas. Let her figure it out.

21-24 Months

Beginning Drawing

Seat your toddler at a table of comfortable height for her. Have sheets of blank paper and a fat pencil or crayons. Tell her to watch you. Make a line, then say, "Can you make a line?" Praise her efforts. Help her hold the crayon correctly. Try making a circle, a "V," and other simple shapes and lines, one at a time, and let her copy you.

Let your child watch while you make a circle, describe your hand motion simply by saying something like "I move my hand around," then give her the pencil and say, "Now you try." Gently move her hand in a circular motion, demonstrate again, and let her try without your help. As your toddler experiences success, do the same for drawing a line and a "V" and any other simple shapes.

Solving New Toys

Keep some toys that you have stored for your toddler and give her one from time to time. Watch her at first and see if she can figure it out. If she is having trouble, give her a clue. For example, say, "Janie, turn it the other way." Resist showing her.

Watch your child when she is in a play group or center where she is not acquainted with the toys. Watch her initiative to see if she has the focus to find out on her own how the toy works.

Give your toddler a new toy and ask simple questions like "Can you make it go?" or "Does it wind?" or "Can you turn it on?" or "Does it need batteries?" Let your toddler watch as you demonstrate or look for ways to make toys or other things work. Talk about what you are trying to do.

Naming Pictures

It's important that your toddler learn about the things in the world, not only for language development, but also for building knowledge. Use picture books, and not only read the stories, but point to the objects in the pictures and name them for her. Let her name them on her own. Check out new books from the library to expand her world.

Use pictures of familiar objects and ask your child to name them and note if she can name at least four.

Keep magazines and picture books handy. After reading a story, go back through the book and name objects in the book. Ask your toddler to point to the object and then name it.

Nesting Toys

Blocks that stack and objects that nest are great educational toys for your toddler. Give your child blocks of different sizes and tell her to build a tower. Watch to see if she learns to put the bigger blocks on the bottom. You can use measuring cups as a nesting toy. Tell her to put them "in" each other. Watch to see if she can figure out the progression. Stacking rings with progressively larger rings are another good toy for learning about sequencing and order. This is a good logic activity.

Have your toddler stack your plastic bowls and cups and aluminum cooking pans so that you can put them away neatly. Start with only two or three items and suggest that she find the biggest one, then the next, then the next. Add more pieces as she learns to compare sizes.

Three-Piece Puzzles

Be sure you get a simple shape puzzle for your toddler. The best ones are durable and made of wood with little handles or knobs on the pieces of simple geometric shapes—circles, squares, and triangles. Show her how to put a piece in the right space and make it a fun game. At this age, she should be able to place at least three pieces correctly.

Give your toddler clues to finding places for puzzle pieces by naming the attributes of a particular puzzle piece. Say, "That piece has corners," have her touch the corners, and ask, "Where is a place that has corners?"

25-30 Months

Waiting

When your toddler comes and interrupts you when you are busy with another task, ask her to wait a minute. It's important for her to realize that she cannot demand your attention on her own timeline all the time. She needs to learn that other people also have timelines. Be firm and tell her to be quiet and wait a minute. Then go back to your task, ignore her pleas for 1 minute, then if she's quiet, give her attention. Eventually, she will understand this, and become more patient.

Begin by saying things like "just a second," hesitate a second or so, then begin to do whatever your toddler wants. After a week or so of this, begin to wait a few more seconds before starting to do what your toddler wants, extending the period of time as she begins to wait. Be sure to reward waiting by drawing attention to her "good waiting" and pointing out that you will do it if she waits. Start being specific about time periods by setting a timer, or showing your toddler on a clock when you will do something. Draw attention to the lapsed period of time.

Understanding Consequences

The most successful means of discipline with a toddler is the use of "logical consequences." At this age, toddlers are learning about the consequences of actions—not just their own actions, but of lots of actions. These consequences and actions can be physical (pulling out a block from a tower results in the tower falling; throwing a rubber ball to the ground will make it bounce; pushing the button on the doorknob will make it lock) or they can be behavioral (when I cry, I get things; when I say "thank you," I get praised; when I pick up the toys, I get to go outside). State these consequences to her when they happen. You must let consequences happen as much as possible and not interfere with this learning.

Building a Tower

Give your toddler an assortment of blocks on a hard floor. Tell her to build a tower. Start building a tower for her, and then let her continue stacking. Have a good laugh when they fall, then try it again as long as her attention holds.

Show your toddler how to build a tower, then let her playfully knock it over. Tell her it is her turn to build and your turn to knock over. Give her only a few blocks to begin with, adding blocks after she is repeatedly successful with just a few.

Scribbling on a Page

Seat your toddler at a table of appropriate height. Give her a blank sheet of paper and a large pencil or large crayons. Draw a simple picture on the paper and let her watch you. Then let her try. If her "scribblings" go off the paper, say, "No, draw on the paper, not on the table," and then guide her hand back to the paper. If she purposely draws off the paper, stop the activity as a natural consequence.

Each time you give your toddler paper and writing tools, tell her to "keep it on the paper." When she marks off the paper, point out where she did it and remind her to "stay on the paper." After a few times of this, have her point out where she went off the paper. After a few more times, tell her "No more drawing if you go off the paper," then take away the tools if she goes off the paper. Give them back to her after a short time and remind her that if she goes off the paper, "no more." Be sure to follow through.

Understanding One

Ask your toddler to bring you *one* of something. Specifically stress the word *one* by holding up one finger, and do not use the word *a*. For example, say, "Janie, please bring me *one* crayon." If she brings more than one or none, repeat the direction, then take her hand and help her pick up *one* and bring it to you.

Have your toddler help you set the table, asking her to bring you *one* spoon. Repeat this, asking for one thing at a time until the table is set. If your toddler brings more than one thing, send her back with the extra, reminding her that you only want one.

31-36 Months

Stringing Beads

Invest in a bead-stringing kit, that contains a lace (cord or shoelace) and easy-to-handle wooden beads (about 1-inch diameter). Sit at a table with your toddler with the beads and lace laid out in front of her. Say, "Janie, let's make a necklace. Can you string the beads with me?" Show her how to hold the lace in one hand, pick up a bead with the other, and thread it. Let her go on her own when she is ready.

Use a shoelace and thread spools, purchased beads, large macaroni, toilet paper tubes cut into threes, or paper cups with holes in the bottom for stringing. Make the shoelace tip stiff with tape or a toothpick taped around the end. Make a bracelet or belt or a decoration to hang.

Beginning Drawing of a Person

Seat your toddler at a table of appropriate height. Give her a blank sheet of paper and a pencil or crayon of appropriate size. Tell her to draw a boy, girl, man, or lady. Watch how she draws. Ask her about her drawing. She should include a head and legs and be able to point them out to you. Praise her for her beautiful picture!

Ask your toddler to draw a picture of you. Ask her to tell you about her drawing. Ask where your head is, and where your legs are.

Building with Blocks

Give your toddler an assortment of blocks, preferably of different sizes. Sit beside her and start building some sort of structure. Talk while you are building. Say, "Let's see, I'm going to build a house. Let's make it tall. I need a wall. Where's the window?" and so forth. Ask her, "What can you build?" Let her go on her own. Ask her questions about it. Praise her creation and tell her how wonderful it is!

Play alongside your preschooler, building something like a roadway or castle, starting in the middle and adding blocks in every direction including up. Talk about what you are adding to your structure, pausing to ask about her building. Ask if she wants to connect her building with yours, then let her if she wants to.

Understanding Directions

Sit on the floor with your toddler and an assortment of blocks, buckets, and other toys. Create tunnels and bridges and other interesting shapes. Use play dinosaurs or other figures for play. Say, "Put the dinosaur on the bridge, Make the dinosaur go over the river," and so on. Use short, similar direction words like *out, in, in front of, behind, through, between,* and *underneath.* If she makes a mistake, show her what the direction means. Practice using these words to describe pictures in books with her.

Use a sturdy chair or go out to a playground. Tell her *under* and point to under the chair and have her move under it. Add *over, on, in front, behind* to the game. As she learns these direction words, stop pointing and let her play, responding to your words. Play using a tube of fabric like a sock with the toe cut out. Play letting her say the words and correcting your wrong moves.

Turning Pages

When you are reading a book with your toddler, let her turn the pages. Always keep a few books out and available for her to read whenever she wants to. Watch as she chooses one and sits down to "read" it. She should turn the book right-side-up, start at the beginning, and turn the pages one-by-one. If she makes a mistake, show her how to start, hold the book right-side up, and turn the pages correctly.

Starting with sturdy cardboard books, then heavy paper books, and finally regular books, let your preschooler turn the pages of books you read to her. While you work on something else, have her turn to a specific picture in a familiar book. Give her plenty of time to turn pages.

37-42 Months

Knowing Boys from Girls

When you are looking at picture books with your preschooler, point out boys and girls. Point out the differences and use examples from the family. "Look at Susie in this picture. Susie is a girl. Mommy is a girl too. I know Susie is a girl because she told me." When she sees pictures of children, ask her if they are boys or girls. Follow the question by asking what makes them look like boys or girls. Avoid sexist statements by saying things like "Usually boys and men don't wear dresses or bows in their hair, so I think that is a girl," or "Drawings of girls sometimes show longer eyelashes."

Begin by correctly identifying girls and boys, men and women in pictures, on TV, and in life. Suggest why you think they are girls or boys. You might say, "I think that is a girl because boys don't usually wear dresses" or "That person's hair is cut really short, like a lot of boys that I know." Be sure to include exceptions to preconceived ideas of what boys and girls or men and women look like and the things that they do. Be sure to include anatomical differences in your identifications, like "That person has larger breasts, so it is probably a woman" or "Boys and men have penises, and girls and women have vaginas."

Counting to Ten

When you have your preschooler's attention, ask her to count with you. First, use your fingers to count to five. Then count to five with her fingers. Help your preschooler practice everyday counting to five, with and without fingers. When she can recite counting to five on her own without fingers, start counting to ten with her. Once again, begin using fingers to help count, then have her keep reciting, using fingers less often.

There are many ways to practice counting. When playing with blocks or other objects, sit with her and count out ten (blocks, dinosaurs, or crayons). You do it, and then ask your preschooler to count.

Televised children's programs and videos reinforce counting. Let her watch these programs, and then continue the counting activity when the video is over. Ask her to recite counting to ten. If she stumbles, help her with the numbers, and then start again.

Sing and chant counting songs and rhymes. Count while doing other things. Begin by just counting for your preschooler, going on to having her say the numbers with you, and moving on to counting alone and giving small hints to the next number.

Using Touch to Recognize Things

Take favorite toys, household objects, and safe tools and place them one at a time in a pillow case or sack when your child isn't watching. Have your preschooler feel the item without looking and try to identify it. Some objects you can "test" are a ball, a carrot, a truck, a doll, and a shoe. The objective is to help your preschooler use all of her senses in exploring the world around her.

Play "close your eyes" by having your preschooler close her eyes and hold out her hands. Place familiar items in her hands, like spoons, forks, cups, coins, and toy cars and have her name the item. Let her keep the items she names and count them up when she is done.

Discussing Pictures

It's a good idea to make regular visits to the public library, or to keep a growing assortment of books available for your preschooler. She should have access to lots of interesting, fun, and educational reading and picture material. There are several children's magazines available that would bring new stimulating material to her on a monthly basis. Visit your public library to peruse them. Take the opportunity to sit with your child and look through books and magazines. Take your time as you read through them, pointing out pictures, and discussing what you see. Later, when you are away from the material you've read together, bring up the topics you discussed again, and see if she remembers what she saw and is interested in talking about it.

Ask your preschooler what she is looking at while she is looking at it. Ask questions about what she describes. If she shows it to you, say something like "Oh, you are looking at Bugs Bunny on TV. Can you say Bugs Bunny on TV?" Once she is telling you what she is looking at, delay your question until she is done looking at it. As your preschooler successfully tells you, delay your questions a little longer each time. With success, start making your questions more vague, like "What did you do today, Did you watch any TV? What books did you look at?" Answer your preschooler's questions about things she sees.

Following Directions

Everyday, give your preschooler directions to follow. Start by giving your preschooler simple one-step directions that are quickly completed, like "Come here," or "Give me a hug." Add more complicated one step directions that take longer to complete. Follow or lead your preschooler, only reminding her of the direction if she gets distracted. Reward your preschooler with simple, natural things like, "We go for a walk when you bring me your coat." Once successful at this, move to two-step directions that are quick to complete and make sense to your preschooler to put together, like, "Get your shoes and your jacket and we will go for a walk" or you might ask her to "Brush your teeth, then comb your hair" or "Find your shoes, then get your school bag." Watch to see if she follows through with both tasks. If she doesn't, state the directions again, and lead her to each task.

43-48 Months

Memory-Matching

There are several picture memory games available for preschoolers that you can purchase or you can easily make your own by cutting out pairs of identical pictures and pasting them on small sheets of paper. Simply place one or two pairs of pictures face down and mix them up on a table or on the floor. Tell your preschooler to turn over two pictures to reveal what's on the other side. As she turns incorrect pictures, ask her what she found before she turns it back. When you call for that picture, remind her that she saw it before, and then say "Can you find it again?" Take turns with her, and she will be challenged to remember where she saw a certain picture so she can turn it over and make a match. Set aside the matching pairs and see who has the most pairs when all the pictures have been matched. Give her another free turn and praise her whenever she finds a match. Add more pictures or matching pictures as your preschooler succeeds. Play with a different deck of cards, matching shapes, colors, or numbers.

Geometric Shapes

Seat your preschooler at a table or desk of appropriate height for her. Have available blank sheets of paper, pencils, and crayons. Draw a circle, a triangle, a rectangle, and a square all on one sheet. As you draw each one, tell her what it is and have her repeat the word. Then point to the shapes in random order and say, "What is this?" If she makes a mistake, tell her the right name. Then tell her to "Point to the triangle" (and then to each of the shapes). Watch to see how she does, and point to the correct shape when she makes a mistake.

Have your preschooler point to circles, rectangles, and triangles she finds around the house, on TV, in books, and on road signs.

Remembering

Give your preschooler a chance to talk about recent events she was involved in. Ask her about what she did earlier in the day, what she saw the day before, and about any new things she might have received. When she spontaneously talks about recent happenings, stimulate her memory even further by asking her a few questions and entering into a discussion about the events.

Ask your preschooler if she did things like brush her teeth, wash her hands, or put away her shoes immediately after she does them. Ask her more detailed questions about what she has done. Once successful at this, delay asking and even instruct her to tell you when she is done, then ask questions. Talk about events that happened earlier in the day and ask if she liked or disliked what had happened. Ask about what she had for breakfast, dinner, or a snack. Wait longer and longer to discuss things that have happened. Finally, ask vague questions like "What was it that we did this morning that you liked so well?" or "Tell me about what you did this morning."

Drawing a Person

Give your preschooler a blank sheet of paper and a pencil or crayon. Tell her to draw a person. It can be anyone she chooses. When she is finished, ask about the parts of the person. As she describes her drawing, note whether she included the head, legs, arms, trunk, and shoulders.

When you are looking at pictures in a book, point to the pictures of people and ask your preschooler to point to the head, arms, hands, feet, legs, knees, stomach, shoulders, nose, eyes, mouth, and hair. Follow up with a drawing activity and ask her to draw a person, then watch to see what she includes in her drawing.

Draw a picture of yourself while your child looks on, naming the body parts as you draw. Include head, arms, legs, torso, and shoulders, and only a few other small details like eyes, mouth, and nose. Have your preschooler draw a self-portrait in the same manner, and say things like "What part are you making now?" Avoid correcting or directing. Praise whatever she draws by displaying it and saying something like, "You drew a nice oval shape for your head."

Drawing Circles

Give your preschooler sheets of blank paper and something to write or draw with (fat crayons, pencils, or markers). Tell her to watch you as you draw a circle. Draw a 3- to 6-inch circle on a blank sheet of paper. Then give her the pencil and guide her hand to help her trace your circle. Then tell her to draw a circle by herself. Let her draw several circles using different colors. Later, show her a circle, and ask her to draw one of her own, without showing her again how to draw it.

Point out a circle shape in a book or magazine and ask your preschooler to "Draw a circle like this one."

49-60 Months

Cutting on a Line

Draw a 2- or 3-inch rather thick line (a wide-tipped marker is perfect) on several pieces of paper, and give your preschooler a small, safe scissors. Tell her to watch you as you cut on the line, and show her how to cut on one of the lines. Then give her one of the papers with a line on it, and tell her to cut on the line. Help her hold the scissors correctly, and tell her about scissors safety. If she goes outside the line, just remind her to cut on the line.

Draw a series of thick parallel lines across a page, spaced about 1 inch apart. Start the lines on one edge of the paper, but stop before reaching the other side. Give your preschooler a blunt-ended scissors that cuts easily and tell her to follow the lines and stop. When she is done, let her wave the fringes in the air, throw the paper up and watch it flutter down.

Knowing Opposites

Using one of your preschooler's books with lots of pictures in it, page through the book and use the pictures to talk about opposites. For example, point to a bug and say, "Look, this bug is not *big*, it is _____." Tell her the word if she does not come up with it. Other opposites to look for are *up/down, top/bottom, long/short, hot/cold, pretty/ugly, in/out, light/dark,* and *soft/hard.* Begin using the term *opposite.* Say, "The opposite of *big* is *little*, the opposite of *hot* is _____. What is the opposite of *in*?" Note that the concept of some of these opposites may still be a little too abstract; so stick to the simplest concepts.

Play the "opposites" game. Take turns naming opposites with your preschooler. First your preschooler names the opposite for a word you name, then she gives you a word and you name the opposite. Play the game pointing to opposites, mimicking opposites, and naming opposites. Ask your librarian to help you find a preschooler's book about opposites.

Knowing About the Seasons

As changes in seasons approach, there are many things you can do to help your preschooler understand and enjoy them. For example, when fall comes, go for a walk and talk about the changing color and falling of the leaves. Remind her that she needs to wear a warmer jacket because it is getting colder. Show her how the birds are flocking to move south for the winter. Have similar discussions and question and answer sessions for each season, not just in the beginning of the season, but all season long. The most important learning about the seasons occurs when time is spent outdoors in nature. Visits to parks, gardens, lakes, and any place where nature's changes can be enjoyed and observed are great educational adventures.

When seasonal holidays approach, it's fun to participate in preparations. Making valentines, watching fireworks, and going to an Easter egg hunt are all activities that mark the changing seasons and holidays in our lives. These experiences can be rich and create wonderful memories that last a lifetime. Family traditions can be established and explained at very early ages, and participation should be automatic.

For each impending season, talk about the changing weather and clothing and about the holidays, and other events that will happen during that season. Make a calendar, give your preschooler magazines, and let her cut out pictures appropriate to the season then paste pictures on the calendar. Make a new calendar season by season or month by month.

Knowing Colors

When you are reading books with your preschooler, use the pictures to talk about colors. At a very early age, show her the basic colors of red, blue, green, and yellow. Have her tell you the color of various pictures, or ask her to point to everything in a picture that is a particular color.

Have your preschooler pick out all the red toys in her collection, then the blue, then the yellow and green. When she brings you something, name the color, then do what she wants or answer her question. When giving directions, use color in your descriptions.

Have your preschooler help to make and sort things by colors (socks, towels, toys, etc.).

Counting Things

Place 10 to 15 pennies and a small bowl on a table. Tell your preschooler to count three pennies and put them in the bowl. If she doesn't, do it yourself, showing her slowly, "one—two—three, that's three pennies. Now you count three pennies." When you feel she is ready, go ahead and show her how to count to five pennies.

Spread an array of toys on the floor in front of your preschooler. Tell her to count three toys and give them to you. Help her if she has trouble.

Ask your preschooler what number of things she wants, like, "How many cookies would you like?" Whatever number she names, have her count with you as you give them to her. If she names more than she is allowed to have, simply say, "How about ..." and count out that many. Place one or two things in front of your preschooler and show her how to point and count. Have her repeat, then give her another number and count again.

61-72 Months

Copying Letters

On a sheet of blank paper, print the capital letters O, V, H, and T about 2 inches high. Seat your preschooler at a desk or table and give her a pencil or marker. Show her your paper with the four letters on it. Point and say, "This is an O. Can you make an O just like this one right here?" Watch to see if she copies the O next to the one you made. Do the same with the other three letters. Praise her efforts and tell her what a big girl she is. Spend a little more time on those letters that cause her difficulty.

Begin by letting your preschooler watch as you make the capital letters O, V, H, and T. As you make them, tell her how you make them, saying something like "I make a line down, then across for a T." Give her your work and let her try. Once she does that well, get a book, magazine, or newspaper, find those letters, circle or highlight them with a marker, and have her copy them.

Counting Fingers

Sit with your preschooler and tell her, "We need to count our fingers." Tell her to watch you as you slowly count each finger up to three. Hold up the three fingers and ask her how many fingers that is. Tell her if she doesn't know. Then help her count three fingers on her hand. When she is ready, count five fingers, and have her do the same.

Matching Numbers and Things

On index cards or small sheets of paper, use a marker to clearly print the numbers from 1 to 10. Seat your preschooler on the floor with an assortment of toys and other objects. Hold up the number 1 for her to see, and say, "This is 1, can you give me *one* ball?" If she doesn't know what to do, then hold up *one* ball, and say, "Look, this is *one* ball." Then proceed to the number 2 and do the same. Go ahead up to number *10*. Then present a number at random, and see if she can count out the correct number of items.

Begin by having your preschooler name numbers she sees printed. Have her name numbers that you write or that you point out or that she sees on things around the house. Once this is mastered, place coins or buttons in three groups, one group with three items and the others with two and four items. Draw a number on a piece of paper and ask your preschooler which group has that number of things.

Sorting Things

Place an assortment of toys and objects of various sizes and colors in front of your preschooler. Tell her to give you all the *red* ones, or all the *little* ones, and so forth. Other activities you can try with your preschooler include sorting by shape, by weight, by feel, or by length. She may even be able to identify objects that don't belong—another important thinking skill.

Have your preschooler organize her toys by sorting them into separate piles, like all the things with wheels in one pile, all the hats in another, and all the books in another. When putting the items away, have her arrange some by color, others by shape, and still others by size.

Pointing to a Number

Write the numbers from 1 to 10 on sheets of paper or notecards. Place a set of ten pennies in front of your preschooler. Count out three pennies and say, "Look. Here are three pennies. Can you show me the number 3?" Then help her point to the number 3. Do the same with all the numbers. Be sure to praise her when she points to the correct numeral.

During television viewing, ask your preschooler to turn the TV to a specific channel. When she finds the correct number, praise her. Say, "Yes, Janie, that's channel 4. See the 4." Then point to it on the TV display.

Have your preschooler find specific numbers in books, magazines, and newspapers. Let her press named numbers to dial the phone, program the microwave, change the TV channel, etc.

11

Activities to Enhance Adapting

It is often said that children develop in spite of our well-intentioned teaching. Often, all we really need to do is to provide ample chances for our children to explore on their own. Below is a laundry list of adaptational activities to introduce to your son or daughter. Consider the list a springboard from which you can launch into your own ideas for enhancing your child's development. Take the ideas listed below and make them work for you, for your child, and for your family. While some ideas may seem simplistic and repetitive, they are perfect for most children. If your child wants to do the same thing over and over, that is perfectly normal and should be encouraged. If your child turns away, struggles, resists, or otherwise indicates she doesn't want to participate, listen to her. Children are notorious for disliking something once, then adoring it the next time, so don't give up—try, try again.

Play is "child's work" and your baby should spend much of her waking alert times in some sort of play. While the play activities listed below are organized into developmental categories, it is important to remember that play in one area develops all areas.

It is important to allow and encourage your child to explore her environment with as much independence and self-motivation as is safe for her age. As your child grows, her need for your supervision, direction, and motivation will vary. You might come to realize that your child resists your attempts to "teach" her. Listen to her. Allow her to explore and learn on her own. Provide the materials and the opportunity. While this independence is important, your child

should never be completely unsupervised or allowed to use toys, tools, or appliances not intended for children her chronological or developmental age.

The most important principle in enhancing the development of adapting skills and independence is experience. You must let your baby move, do things for herself, and explore her environment. Parents who help their child do too much or who help too often are impeding their child's' growth and development. From the earliest stages in infancy, place your child on a blanket on the floor or in a "playpen." Let her move, wiggle, roll, stretch, and reach. As she becomes a toddler, she will wear you out with her awkward attempts to do things for herself. Your role is to provide a safe, supervised environment for her to explore, and then let her go! Infants and toddlers who are allowed to be physically active and do things for themselves enter school with a high degree of self-esteem and confidence, as well as good coordination, strength, and stamina.

The activities below link directly to the items in the checklist. If your child has scored low on a particular motor behavior that you think she should be able to do, study the activity in the list below and incorporate it into your child's routine. Feel free to adapt or expand the activity to suit your home and situation. Most of all, have fun with these activities! Although they are designed to practice and reinforce specific movements, they cannot be successful until they're brought to life; only you can make the learning process fun.

0-4 Months

Waiting to be Fed

When your baby is fussing, delay her feeding just a few minutes. Give her plenty of attention, but try not to feed her outside of her eating schedule, by delaying her feeding each time just a few minutes to develop a healthy eating pattern.

Always hold and cuddle your baby while she eats. Stroke and kiss her hands and legs. Pat her bottom, rub her back, and stroke her cheek. This is a great time to let yourself admire your baby, and she will sense your love and attention by how you handle her.

Anticipating Feeding

Seat your baby strapped safely in an infant seat in the kitchen while you prepare her meal. Let her hear the refrigerator door, the microwave, and other preparation sounds as you get her food ready. Talk to her, saying things like "Are you hungry? You've been such a good girl," and so forth.

Acknowledge your baby's presence clearly and frequently by talking to her face. Make sure she can see you. This will help her wait to be fed. Place your baby where she can see you prepare to feed her. Tell her what you are doing, using the same sort of phrasing and words to describe food and feeding.

React to your baby's excitement at feeding preparations by telling her she is right, she is going to get to eat soon. Say things like "Its coming," "I'm getting it," "Supper's here."

Being Aware of Strangers

Have visitors come into your home while the baby is alert and seated where she can watch the "action." Watch her reaction to strangers. She may grow quiet, frown, stare intently, or otherwise behave differently when approached by someone who is not familiar to her.

Expose your baby to those she doesn't know. Acknowledge when she frowns or turns away or studies that person intently. Ask her "Who is that?"—then tell her. Reassure her that it is okay to turn away, frown, and study people she doesn't know.

When your baby awakes, let her know you are present by talking to her, moving into her line of vision, and then picking her up. Watch her reaction when she notes your presence. She should either quiet her body or show excitement when you approach her.

Eating Once During the Night

Ease into once-a-night feedings by briefly comforting your baby if she wakes after her one nighttime feeding. Delay nighttime feedings by waiting a minute or two to see if your baby really wakes up.

Try a pacifier to help your baby wait a little longer between feedings.

Responding to Parents

Spend extra time bonding with your baby. Feeding time, bath time, and diaper times are great times to touch, cuddle, and generally "love up" your baby. The more time you spend with your baby, the sooner and more evident will be your baby's response to your presence.

5-8 Months

Eating Baby Food

Most parents introduce baby food at this age. Follow your health care provider's instructions in introducing baby foods at regular mealtimes.

Eating Finger Foods

Check with your health care provider about introducing safe finger foods like baby toast, teething biscuits, or food morsels. Place only a few pieces of finger foods at a time within your baby's reach and watch closely for any signs of choking.

Small slices of banana or graham crackers are examples of finger foods that may be permissible to feed your baby. Be sure to talk with your health care provider about finger foods that are appropriate for your baby to feed herself. Place the food pieces on her high chair tray in front of her at mealtime. Move her hand to the food and help her pick it up, then guide her hand to her mouth so she can eat it. Encourage her to eat more, and watch to see if she picks up the food on her own.

Take special care to prevent choking by supervising your baby closely as she learns to eat finger foods. Take an infant first aid course.

Feeding Herself the Bottle

Place your baby's hands on the bottle while you hold her for feeding.

There are specially made plastic bottles that are designed to be easy for your baby to hold during drinking. With milk in the bottle, and your baby in position ready to drink, place the bottle in her hands and guide it to her mouth. Then let go and see if she continues to hold it. Gradually let go more and more until she is able to hold onto the bottle for longer periods. Let your baby play with her bottle while you hold her.

Refusing Things

You may notice while you are washing your baby's face, changing her, or feeding her, that she acts very stubborn and refuses to cooperate with you. She may turn her head away from the spoon or make a fuss when you are bathing her, showing her own independence. These are good signs, but you must be firm with her about cooperating, and continue the activity until you are finished. Do not, however, force your baby to eat if she absolutely refuses.

Whenever possible and practical, respect your baby's refusal of food, toys, or activities. Say things like "You don't want it? Okay?"

Attaching to Parents

Leave your baby in the care of trusted others from time to time. You may notice her crying or being unhappy when you leave, and very happy or very cold toward you when you return. These are signs of attachment to you. She needs to feel secure knowing that you are coming back. When you return, give her attention by saying things like, "Hi, Janie. Did you miss me? I missed you too. Did you act good while I was gone?" and so forth.

9-12 Months

Holding a Cup for Drinking

Give your baby sips from a cup starting as soon as she can sit upright on her own. Let her explore empty cups, and those with just a very little liquid. Encourage her to hold her own bottle and praise her efforts to control the cup you hold for her.

Specially designed "tippy" or "sippy" cups are great for teaching your baby to hold her own cup to drink. Put some milk or juice in the cup, then guide her hands toward holding it and bringing it to her mouth so she can drink. Then let her manipulate it on her own.

Keeping Herself Busy

When you sit your baby down to play, put toys around her so she must reach for, crawl to, pick up, and manipulate them. Give your baby safe new and interesting toys to explore. Step back and let her go at it while you look on. Don't immediately pick her up or go to her once she loses interest; wait to see if she finds something to do. As she begins to occupy herself, extend the time period you wait to help her find something new to do. Stay nearby without interacting with her, and let her play safely on her own. Make a mental note or set a timer to determine just how long she will occupy herself with the toys. At this age, she should be able to keep herself busy with one or more activities for 10 minutes or longer.

Helping Get Dressed

Dress your baby when she is happy and not distracted. As you dress your baby, give her the chance to "help" you. Hold the arm hole out, encouraging her to put her arm in. Tell her to pull her pants up, and help her when she needs it. Tell her what you want her to do when you are dressing her, like "push your arm through, " then push her elbow to help straighten her arm into the sleeve. Praise her when she cooperates. Encouraging her to a share of the work in getting dressed helps her learn to be independent in dressing.

Break the task of dressing into little "chunks." Say something like "Step into your pants by lifting up a foot," or "Put your foot into the hole, then pull your pants on," instead of saying, "Put your pants on."

Holding a Spoon

During mealtime, give your baby a spoon. You may use a specially designed baby spoon that's easy for her to hold. While she's holding the spoon, guide her into putting some food on the spoon, and bringing it to her mouth. Then let her try on her own. Your baby may not actually use the spoon to eat, or may use it sporadically or messily, but she will hold it in her hand while eating.

Put a spoon near your baby during meals and snack times. Let her see you holding eating utensils. Show her how to use a spoon. Place the spoon on her tongue and comment on its shape and how cool and smooth it feels.

Choosing Toys

During playtime, have an assortment of toys available and accessible to your baby. Watch to see which toys she chooses on her own. Store toys on sturdy, safe shelves that your baby can see and reach. At this age, your baby is beginning to express her own preferences—a sign of developing independence.

13-16 Months

Asking for Help

As your baby is playing, she may encounter a problem with a toy. Maybe it is broken or she can't get it to work. When she begins to express her frustration, tell her to come to you, to bring the toy, and that you will see if you can fix it. Watch to see if she begins to ask for help on her own.

Tell your baby when things are broken and explain when you have fixed something. Build a tower of blocks, let her break it, then tell her you will fix it.

Sitting Down for Awhile

It's a good idea to have special furniture available for your baby to get into on her own. For example, a chair just her size will give her a place to go to. Sit near her as you seat her in her chair, and occupy her attention with a toy or with conversation. See if you can get her to sit there a for a minute or two. Then watch to see if she goes to the chair on her own, and sits there for a little while.

Give your baby the time to crawl into a chair, turn around, and sit down. Put a favored toy or item on the back of the chair. Sit on a chair and let your baby crawl up on your lap and sit down.

No More Bottle

Check with your pediatrician about keeping your baby's bottle out of sight during the day, and letting your baby obtain most of her nutrition from her baby food. The doctor might recommend an evening or morning bottle, but with less liquid or a pacifier instead.

With your pediatrician's advice, begin to replace bottle feeding with solid food and drinking cups. Distract your baby from the bottle by introducing new activities that she cannot do with the bottle. When your baby puts her bottle down to do something else, put it away until she "asks" for it, then delay giving it back to her by giving her a sip from a cup or playing with her.

You might begin to give your baby a "cuddly" object like a favorite stuffed toy or blanket for her to hold when she is put down for naps or at night.

Wanting a Diaper Change

When you see that your baby is uncomfortable, is walking "funny," or is pointing to her diaper, say, "Janie, should we change your diaper?" Then go ahead and change her, saying something like "Let's get rid of that icky diaper. Yuck! You're a big girl for telling me. There, doesn't that feel better? Now you're all clean."

Play the diaper check game: every hour or so announce "diaper check" and check your baby's diaper for wetness and soiling. After checking, announce what you have found—"all dry," "smelly," "dirty," "wet," etc. Use the same words to describe the diaper's condition so that your baby learns to associate the words with the feeling in her diaper. When you change her diaper, announce "all dry."

Expressing Wants

When your baby wants something, she may come to you and tug on you, cry, scream, or make a fuss. Tell her to stop and tell you what she wants. If she gives one word, like cracker, say, "Cracker? Can you say cracker, please?" Pause for her to calm down and say what she wants. "Okay. You want a cracker. Here you are."

Acknowledge your child's demands and give her the things that are appropriate. Give your child a choice between two items or activities whenever possible. The natural consequence of her choice is being satisfied or disappointed in her choice.

17-20 Months

Eating Independently

When it is mealtime, seat your toddler in her chair, with her bib, the food in her dish or plate, and her spoon and "tippy" cup. Don't put the food directly in front of her until the family is all seated and ready to eat. Then put the food in front of her and tell her to go ahead and eat. If she acts like she wants you to feed her, don't. Just point to the food and tell her to eat, and let her feed herself. Point out how the others feed themselves.

Encourage your toddler to pretend to feed herself and her toys. Provide safe dishes, spoons and forks. Prepare a meal or two that your toddler loves so that she will be likelier to eat without help. Although it will be messy, let her try to eat the foods you serve yourself. Always have her try to eat one or two bites without your help.

Leading Others to Things

When it seems as if your toddler has something to show you, get her to take your hand and lead you to it. Go with her and see what it is she wants you to see.

Play a game with your toddler by announcing "take me to your room," then follow your toddler to her room. Play this game with rooms, people, and objects.

Helping to Get Dressed

As you dress your toddler, give her opportunities to help. Have her get clothing from an accessible drawer, step into her pants, put her arms up, or partially put some of her clothing on herself. Praise her when she does help, and encourage her to do a little more each time.

Name articles of clothing, and have your toddler name them with you, then ask "Can you bring your shirt?" or "Can you put your leg in here?" Try some silly requests like "Can you put your shirt in your ear?"

Putting on Shoes

Your toddler may actually enjoy taking her shoes off, giving you lots of opportunity to teach her to put them back on. Encourage her to put on her own shoes. She may get them on the wrong feet, and she won't be able to tie the laces, but praise her for getting them on her feet on her own.

Provide easy slip-on shoes or slippers and show your toddler how to put them on. Praise her when she puts her toes in, then help her with the rest. Let your toddler put on oversized shoes for play, and let her put your shoes on you. Give her plenty of time to try.

Zipping and Unzipping

On your toddler's jacket, you can start the zipper, and then let her pull it up. Let your toddler work a well-greased, easily operating larger jacket zipper, holding the top and bottom for her. You can also start the pull down, then let her pull the zipper down the rest of the way. You can even have her practice on your jacket, purse, or gym bag.

21-24 Months

Asking for Food and Drink

When your toddler clearly wants something to eat or drink, don't give it to her until she asks nicely. Say, "Janie, do you want some juice? Say, Can I have some juice, please?" Then pause for her to try to say, "Juice, please." When she spontaneously asks for something and says "please," be sure to praise her, and acknowledge her request.

Acknowledge your toddler's indications that she wants something, and if at all possible, give it to her. Say the name of the item, then tell her, "Now you say (name the item again)." In the beginning, accept any utterance or acknowledgment and give her the item. Once she begins saying a few words, require a little better answer before giving her the item. Once you are sure she can vocalize her wants and needs, require that she use her own words.

Putting Toys Away

Make it a routine that when your toddler is finished playing, she is to pick up her toys and put them away. Be sure you have an easy, convenient storage system for your toddler to use, like low, spacious shelving so she can easily see and choose her toys. When it is time to put them away, pick up a toy or two, and tell her to "Put the toys away," or begin specifically, "Pick up the ball, and put it on the shelf."

Make it easy for your toddler to put away her toys by providing low shelving. Direct her clean up efforts by asking her things like "Where is your truck?" When she locates it, add, "Get your truck and bring it to me." That accomplished, add, "Get your truck, bring it to me, and help me put it on the shelf." Once she is successfully helping, progress to "Clean up the toys by putting the truck on the shelf." Reward her by letting her pick her snack, a book to read, a song to sing, etc.

Eating Table Food

With your pediatrician's approval, move away from baby food, and begin to give your toddler table food. Be sure you follow a healthy diet according to your pediatrician's guidelines. Cut up table food into bite-size pieces as needed. Carefully supervise the size of her bites, then see if she can chew more slowly than you can, or chew until you count to five. Play "yum-yum" by having your toddler put down her spoon and rub or pat her tummy after each bite while she is chewing.

Sharing Attention

When you are in a conversation with someone else, and your toddler wants your attention, tell her to wait a minute until you are finished. Then turn away from her and continue your conversation, ignoring any other pleas your toddler may make. After a minute has passed, turn to her and give her attention. She must begin to realize that you have other things to attend to, and that she must share your attention with your other demands.

Start your toddler doing something she likes to do that she is able to do safely without your full attention—building with blocks, looking at books, playing with a toy, etc. Once involved, leave her to play for a few seconds, and as soon as she starts to be distracted, redirect her interest and leave again. Continue to extend the periods of time you share your attention with your toddler and another activity.

Opening Doors

Show your toddler how to turn door knobs and open appropriate doors. both inward and outward, on her own. Stand with your toddler on the side of a door so that it pushes open. Put a toy on the other side. Place your toddler's hands on top of the knob so that gravity will help her to turn it. Allow her to enjoy the noise the clicking door knob makes. Push against the closed door when she turns the knob so that the door opens. Next time, move her or place her so that she leans against the door making it open, then let her practice.

25-30 Months

Putting on Simple Clothing

Encourage your toddler to put on simple clothing without your help. She should be able to pull on elastic-waisted pants, loose-fitting shirts, jackets, and shoes without fastening, and other simple garments. Tell her to put them on herself, and then praise her when she does. Complete the final adjusting and fastening yourself.

Keep the clothes your toddler is allowed to choose and get for herself in low, accessible uncrowded areas. Lay her clothes in a trail on the floor in the order they are to be put on. Have your toddler start the more difficult items, then finish them with your help.

For difficult jackets and button down shirts, teach your toddler the "flip." Have her kneel down and lay the article of clothing front side up, with the neck opening at her knees. Have her put her arms straight into the arm holes (no crossing over), then slip the article of clothing over her head.

Washing Hands

Put a low, sturdy stool in front of the bathroom sink so that your toddler can reach the faucet. Show her how to turn on the faucet, put her hands under the running water, use soap and rub her hands together, rinse, and then dry. She may need help adjusting the water temperature and making a lather, but praise her for any steps she completes on her own. Send her to the sink to wash her hands on her own at relevant times.

Let your toddler wash your hands, instructing her to wash the tops, the palms, and between each finger—her hands will become clean too.

Asking to Go to the Bathroom

When your toddler gives nonverbal indications that she needs to go to the bathroom, ask her, "Janie, do you need to use the toilet?" If she says "yes," then tell her to say, "Toilet" or "I need to go potty," or some phrase to let you know that she needs to go. When she makes motions as if she is having a bowel movement, say, "Time to use the potty" and take her. Praise her when she comes up to you on her own and tells you that she needs to use the bathroom. Use the same phrase and words each time you refer to urination and bowel movements when talking to your toddler.

Helping to Brush Teeth

During your toddler's morning ritual and bedtime bathroom routine, when it is time for brushing teeth, encourage her to do as much of the process on her own as she can. Move a low, sturdy stool in front of the bathroom sink, so she can reach the faucet and the countertop. Place her toothbrush in a reachable holder and the toothpaste in a location that's easy for her to reach. Show her how to wet her toothbrush, open the toothpaste container, put toothpaste on the brush, and then brush her teeth. Help her where needed, but praise her for those steps she does or tries on her own. You may need to finish the brushing. Most importantly, you want to see her cooperate during the entire process.

Play a game of inspecting your toddler's teeth. Have her show you after she has brushed each surface (inside uppers, inside lowers, top lowers, top uppers, outside uppers, outside lowers).

Following Routines

Be sure to follow the same routine for mealtimes and bedtimes. Help your toddler wash her hands before and after meals, help to clear the table and clean up after meals, get ready to take naps, and do bathroom routines to prepare for bedtime. You may need to remind her, "What do we do before we go to bed?" Praise her for taking initiative to start some of the routine tasks on her own.

Take photos of your toddler in her routines and place them in order in a book or on a poster or on the refrigerator. Talk about your routines in simple phrases using the same words each time.

31-36 Months

Starting Conversations

Let your toddler start conversations on her own. Have a "tea party" or "juice break" where you sit down with her at a table and talk. When she begins talking about something, converse with her and help her keep the conversation going. She should be sharing her experiences, discussing her plans, and expressing her wishes with you and others. During the conversation, no matter how brief, watch to see if she can follow the train of thought and answer related questions.

When your preschooler talks, stop, squat down to her eye level, and listen intently. Try not to interrupt or comment—just listen. Praise her by saying something like "That is a good idea," "I like when you tell me about. . . ," "Tell me more" or "What else?"

Being Orderly

Help your toddler learn to be orderly by making picking up part of the daily routine. When she leaves her toys to come to eat, tell her to pick up her toys. Do the same before leaving the house, going down for a nap, or going to bed. Help her put things in their proper place. Show her how to "straighten" things and pick up things other than just toys. For example, she can put the dogs toys in the dog's bed, or pick up a magazine left on the floor. Praise her when she initiates straightening things up.

Give your preschooler spaces of her own to arrange as she likes or needs—a toy shelf or two; a drawer; her own closet hooks for coat, shoes and bag; or an arts and crafts box. Make sure she has plenty of room to fit all her things in their place and watch as she places them. Encourage her to put things in the same place every time.

Being Safe

As she develops, let your toddler know which situations are safe, and which ones are not. Always hold her hand when you walk across the street, teaching her never to step out into the street without an adult or without looking first. Show her that the stove and fireplace are hot, and that she must not touch them. When in a parking lot or other location where there are cars, teach her to stay away from moving cars or bikes, and never to leave your supervision or wander. Praise her if she takes precautions on her own.

Keep the rules simple, like "You must hold my hand in the store" or "If we lose each other, go to another mommy with children." Rehearse what you want your preschooler to do. Be ready to strictly enforce consequences for unsafe behavior, like leaving the store immediately to sit in the car, or not crossing the street but returning home.

Taking Turns

There are many occasions that are ideal for teaching your toddler to wait her turn. At the dinner table, teach her to wait her turn before the food is passed to her. If someone is in the bathroom, she must wait until they are finished. If she is playing with other children, encourage her to wait in line before she gets to go down the slide. If she pushes in front of others or demands to be first, reprimand her, take her to her place or to the end of the line, and say something like "Janie, it's not your turn. Wait a few minutes and then it will be your turn. Wait nicely right here." Take turns at everything—placing blocks on a tower, stirring up a cake, taking bites of food and talking. At first, keep each turn very brief, and as she gets better at taking turns, make each turn a little longer. Use a timer to time longer turns.

Choosing Clothes

It's a good idea to store your toddler's clothes in a location where she can reach them and put them away. Either use lower drawers in a dresser, or install a low clothes pole in the closet with hangers that are easy for her to reach. There are terrific storage bins ideal for storing children's things. When it is time to get dressed, tell your toddler to choose her clothes. Tell her, for example, to get some underwear, a pair of socks, a pair of pants, and then a shirt. Watch to see what her preferences are. You may find her expressing her opinion with certain colors, fabrics, or styles. It's important, at times, to agree with her selections, even though they may not be the best match, and even if she wore them the day before (as long as they're still clean).

Purchase or make coordinated clothing for your preschooler and let her put together her own outfits. Bring your preschooler on one or two single-purpose short shopping trips to pick out a few pieces of clothing and let her choose two to three things you have agreed are appropriate.

37-42 Months

Dressing Independently

During dressing time, establish a routine where your preschooler selects her clothes, lays them out, and then dresses herself. You may want to be there to remind her about the order of things. She should be able to put on her own underwear, pants, socks, shoes, and shirt. Fastenings may still be too difficult for her, so you may need to tie shoes; fasten buttons, hooks or snaps; and start zippers. Praise her efforts as she performs more and more of the dressing on her own.

Make sure your preschooler's clothing is roomy and easy for her to put on. Show her step-by-step how to put on her shoes, pants, and underclothing. Use the same simple phrases and key words, like "loosen the laces, and pull the tongue up," then move on to reminders like "laces, tongue," and finally no reminders.

Undressing Independently

At bedtime, bath time, or other times for undressing, encourage your preschooler to take her own clothes off. She should be able to completely disrobe, and during the process, put clothes where they belong. For example, when she takes her socks and underwear off, show her how to put them in the laundry basket or hamper. Praise her for undressing herself, and only help her with tricky fastenings as needed.

Make a game for your preschooler's undressing by setting the timer or counting and seeing if she can "beat the clock," or let her set the timer or determine the count. Give her plenty of time to work on getting undressed and resist helping. For the most difficult items, have her start or finish taking them off.

Eating Independently

During mealtime, your preschooler should be able to completely feed herself. She should be able to keep her food on her plate, get the food to her mouth without making a mess, and drink liquids without spilling. At the end of the meal, her face should be fairly clean. If she is having trouble or protests in feeding herself, don't feed her. Let her learn that to eat, she must feed herself. She may not clean her plate and eat all of her food, but that's okay, as long as she did eat some. If she puts the utensils down and starts to use her fingers with foods that should be eaten with a spoon or fork, remind her, give her the spoon or fork, and tell her to use them.

Require no spills or allow only one or two, then reward your preschooler by taking her to eat with a friend, to a picnic, or to a restaurant.

Separating from Parents

Leave your preschooler with responsible caretakers from time to time. Establish a regular "good-bye routine" with your preschooler. Talk about the routine before it happens, practice it, then do it. Ignore any fussing or things outside your prearranged parting routine. A good routine might include a kiss, a hug, a good-bye rhyme like "see you later alligator," and a wave from the window. Make it quick, firm, and consistent.

When you leave your preschooler, she should accept that you will return, and should not make a fuss. If she does have a tantrum, complete your good-bye routine, however brief, and leave. If you give her attention, you will be re-inforcing her tantrum behavior, and you will be late for your appointment. Make your departure matter-of-fact. Tell her you're going to the store for a little while, and that so-and-so will be caring for her. Tell her to have a happy time while you're gone and that you'll be back in a little while. Give her a hug and a kiss and then leave. When you return, remind her that you came back as promised and give her your attention.

Focusing on Tasks

Provide your preschooler with toys and activities that will captivate her attention. Building blocks, interlocking blocks, coloring books and crayons, farm animals and dinosaurs, among other toys your preschooler enjoys, should be made available to her for her selection. When she gets into an activity, let her play on her own. Don't tiptoe around her, but go about your daily tasks. At this age, she should be able to block out distractions and continue to focus on her activity.

Give your preschooler puzzles or chores at which she has proven successful. Set her up to work on them, explaining that you will not be able to help her. Try to create a quiet place in a restricted spot, like at the kitchen table, without the TV or radio on. Time how long she works on her project before asking for attention, looking around, or stopping. Direct her attention back to the activity, set the timer for a little longer, and tell her to work on it without stopping until the timer goes off. When she has finished, reward her by giving her your full attention, letting her choose her next activity, and discussing how good it feels to finish. Build on her time a little each day.

43-48 Months

Putting on Shoes

When your preschooler is dressing herself, you may need to help her put her shoes on the right feet. Show her how to place her shoes on the floor in the correct order, and then to put them on the correct feet. If she gets them mixed up, ask her if she feels that they are wrong, and then tell her to switch her shoes. She should be learning to put them on correctly.

Label your preschooler's shoes as left or right with her permission and help. Establish left and right feet using different colored socks, a piece of tape, a special bandage, a rub-on tattoo, etc. Use matching marks on shoes. Point out how a left shoe looks a little different than a right shoe and have your preschooler touch and feel the parts that feel different. Discuss how shoes on the wrong feet feel. Trace your preschooler's shoes, then her feet inside those tracings on a mat or paper. Encourage her to use her foot mat when putting her shoes on.

Eating with Utensils

Provide your preschooler with both a spoon and a fork during mealtime. Show her when to use a fork and when to use a spoon. Praise her when she uses them successfully without spilling.

Have your preschooler set the table with forks and spoons. Let her choose which utensil to use for various foods. Have her practice holding utensils like she would a pencil, marker, or crayon. Comment on correct use. Play "What's wrong?" and use poor table manners including incorrect use of forks and spoons. Let her show how to do it correctly.

Going to the Bathroom Independently

When your preschooler indicates that she needs to use the bathroom, tell her to go ahead, encouraging her to get started or go on her own. You may need to help unfasten some clothing, but let her go on her own, close the door, and wash her hands. She may need to be reminded to flush the toilet and wash and dry her hands when she is finished.

Establish a regular routine to follow each time your preschooler uses the toilet, like "Close the door, lift the toilet lid, pull down pants to knees, sit, use the potty, take three sheets of toilet paper, wipe from front to back, put paper in the toilet, flush, wash hands, dry hands, turn out light." Post pictures for each part of the routine. Turn the longer description of the routine into single reminder words. Rehearse the reminder words throughout toilet training and into supervised toileting, then after each request to use the toilet.

Doing Household Chores

Make a calendar or a chore chart for your preschooler and any other children in the house. Use a sticker, photo, or cut-out magazine picture to show your preschooler what her chore is. You may want to rotate the chore each week or each month. Chores for your preschooler might include clearing dishes from the table, picking up food from the floor, setting the table, collecting dirty clothes, dusting, and so forth. Praise her efforts when she does her chores well and initiates them on her own.

Make a chore list containing a few easy chores for your preschooler. Let her chose her chore for the week. Good chores for a preschooler include: pulling the covers up on her bed, picking up specific types of toys (all the stuffed animals, all the trucks and cars, etc.), setting the cups on the table for meals, clearing the flatware, putting clean flatware away, and dusting specific pieces of furniture. First chores should be daily. Once your preschooler can do one chore daily, add another. Include rewards for remembering chores without being told by placing stars on the chart.

Helping with Meals

It's not too early for your preschooler to help prepare simple meals. She can get the bread and peanut butter for sandwiches, stir the macaroni and cheese, put the cheese on the bread, put bread in the toaster, or other similar meal preparation tasks.

Start by having your preschooler get the needed pans, pots, and food needed to prepare meals. Supply your preschooler with a cook's hat and apron to make cooking fun. Let her add ingredients, stir, spread, etc.

49-60 Months

Washing Hands and Face

In the morning, after outdoor play, and at night, show your preschooler how to wash her face and hands. Show her how to get a washcloth, wet it, lather it up, wash her face and hands, then rinse, dry, and put the washcloth and towel away. After showing her, reduce your supervision a little more each time, until she does it without verbal clues or your supervision. She should be able to clean her face and hands completely by herself.

Use a tear-free soap or shampoo in a "soft soap" dispenser and show your child how to use one squirt. Let her practice by giving you one squirt when you wash your hands. Have a specific routine for washing, like "Wet hands; turn water off; rub hands; hands to cheeks, chin, then forehead, making little circles; rinse hands; cup water; and rinse face four times."

Getting Completely Dressed

When it is time for your preschooler to get dressed, be sure she has selected what she is going to wear, then leave the room and let her dress herself. She should now be putting on all of her own clothes—her socks, underwear, shirt, pants, jacket, and be able to fasten buttons, snaps, and zippers—all on her own without any help. Compliment her on how nice she looks when she is all dressed.

Try to create a motivating reason for your child to get dressed, like going somewhere she wants to go, doing something, etc. Supervise your child's dressing, only announcing what article of clothing to put on, and give her plenty of time to put it on to her satisfaction. Having your child dress in a room away from you while you work on something else will reduce your urge to help her get dressed. When your child asks for help, give her minimal assistance and only if she has started to put on the article of clothing.

Wanting Privacy

When your preschooler is using the bathroom, encourage her to do so privately. Tell her to close the door and use the bathroom by herself. She may be ready for this privacy and not want you or anyone else in the bathroom with her—a normal stage in developing a sense of self.

Establish things that are to be done in private. Add "closing door" to bathroom routines. Knock on closed doors before opening and checking on your child. Comments like "Oh, you need your privacy" or "Please do that in private" or "I know you need your privacy when you close the door" all help to establish bathroom privacy. Announce to others that your child needs her privacy.

Pouring Liquids

Except for large gallon jugs, your preschooler should be able to pour herself a glass of water, juice, or milk with little spilling. Let her have the opportunity to fill glasses at the dining table for others to give her practice in pouring.

Give your child plastic pitchers and cups to use in the bathtub. Make marks in the cup and have her fill to specific lines. Move to filling cups with tap water for getting her own drinks of water. Introduce pouring from juice and milk containers when they are at least half empty. Have her stand to pour, show her where to place her hands, and hold the cup for her. Do this often at first, and give her lots of tries close together at pouring. As her skill improves, reduce your help and supervision. Requiring your preschooler to clean up her spills is a natural consequence and will encourage her to do things carefully.

Completing Projects

Give your preschooler projects to complete. For example, tell her to straighten up and clean her room, giving her some specifics, like "make the bed, put your clothes and toys away, clean the shelf, and vacuum." If she quits before the job is finished, tell her to go back and not leave the room until she is done. When she indicates she's done, look it over and praise her for starting and finishing the job and doing such good work. Try other projects like building a tower, doing a sewing card, completing a puzzle, or coloring a picture. Encourage her to stick with the project until she is completely finished, to help her get a sense of independence in tackling and finishing a project.

Give your child a choice of activities, like a simple puzzle, art project, cleaning job, building project, and explain that she must work on it without your help and needs to clean up afterwards. Give her simple starting suggestions and ask her something like "Now what?" then leave the area and let her work telling her to come get you when she is finished with a certain step. When she does, comment on her project. If she has not cleaned up, tell her she is not done and ask her what is left. Do not allow her to do anything else until she has completed the project. Display completed projects for all to admire.

61-72 Months

Agreeing to Go to Bed

Set a regular bedtime for your preschooler. Help her learn to read the clock so she is able to recognize when it is bedtime. When it is time, point to the clock and say something like, "Look Janie, it's 8 o'clock, time for bed. Go and get ready for bed and I'll be there to say goodnight in about 5 minutes." When you go to "tuck her in" or to read her a book, praise her for being so good, for brushing her teeth, washing up, getting her pajamas on, putting her clothes away, and climbing into bed.

Establish a bedtime routine with clear consequences, like "Children who go to bed immediately after being told get to keep their light on to read a book" or "If you do not go to bed when you are told, I will not sing you your song."

Crossing the Street

Go for walks in a safe area with your preschooler. Show her how to stop, look, and listen before crossing a street, and how to read stoplights and other traffic symbols and signs. When she has proven reliable, allow her to walk next to you, showing safe behavior. Send her a few feet ahead of you, and when you are comfortable, watch to see if she crosses the street safely.

Pretend crossing the street using your hallways, the sidewalk, or other paths. Pretend you are a car or truck or bus while your child tries to cross the street. You can add tape on the ground to mark cross walks, as well as construction paper or flashlight signals and toy cars to make it more realistic for your preschooler.

Tying Shoes

Show your preschooler how to tie her shoes. Encourage her to try to tie them by herself. You may need to tighten them or "double-bow" them so they stay tied, but let her do the tying, even though it may be easier and faster if you do it. Also teach her how to lace a new pair of shoes, then let her do it when the next opportunity arises, even if it's for another family member.

Unlace some shoes and ask for your child's help in lacing them up. Be sure to thank her for her help. Recite a little rhyme or the simplified steps each time you tie your own or your child's shoes. Start by having your child do the first step in tying, adding steps as she learns earlier ones. Tie her shoes slowly for her from behind so that your hands move like hers will. Let her put her hands on top of yours while you tie her shoes so that she feels how your hands move.

Bathing and Showering

Show your preschooler how to shower and take baths by herself. Show her how to adjust the shower, how to wash her hair and her body, and how to rinse off before turning the water off or draining the tub. If bathing, show her how to fill the bathtub, test the water temperature, get in safely, wash herself and her hair, rinse off, empty the tub, and get out safely. Let her shower and bath in privacy.

Have your child show you the steps to bathing a few times. When you are confident that she knows them, leave the room and have her call out to you each step as she does them. After a few times, let her bathe herself, simply checking with her that she has done all the steps. If you suspect she has skipped a step or two, try not to ask "Did you wash your face?" but simply comment that her face is still dirty, show her in the mirror, and have her repeat that step.

Brushing Teeth

At least twice a day, your preschooler should be brushing her teeth. Watch to be sure she brushes all her teeth and takes her time to do so thoroughly. You may need to brush alongside her and show her how to brush correctly. She should be putting her toothpaste on the brush on her own, brushing completely, spitting, rinsing, and then putting everything away.

Have your child watch you brush your teeth and let her inspect your work. Ask her if you've done a good job. Have her brush your teeth and comment on the parts she brushes thoroughly.

12

Activities to Enhance Growing

It is often said that children develop in spite of our well-intentioned teaching. Often, all we really need to do is to provide ample chances for our children to explore on their own. Below is a laundry list of growth-enhancing activities to introduce to your son or daughter. Consider the list a springboard from which you can launch into your own ideas for enhancing your child's development. Take the ideas listed below and make them work for you, for your child, and for your family. While some ideas may seem simplistic and repetitive, they are perfect for most children. If your child wants to do the same thing over and over, that is perfectly normal and should be encouraged. If your child turns away, struggles, resists, or otherwise indicates she doesn't want to participate, listen to her. Children are notorious for disliking something once, then adoring it the next time, so don't give up—try, try again.

Play is "child's work" and your baby should spend much of her waking alert times in some sort of play. While the play activities listed below are organized into developmental categories, it is important to remember that play in one area develops all areas.

It is important to allow and encourage your child to explore her environment with as much independence and self-motivation as is safe for her age. As your child grows, her need for your supervision, direction, and motivation will vary. You might come to realize that your child resists your attempts to "teach" her. Listen to her. Allow her to explore and learn on her own. Provide the materials and the opportunity. While this independence is important, your child should never be completely unsupervised or allowed to use toys, tools or appliances not intended for children her chronological or developmental age.

The most important factors for enhancing healthy growth are regular physical activity, a nutritionally balanced diet, and an emotionally functional, happy household. You must let your baby move, crawl, and physically explore her environment, letting her be active every day. Parents who carry their babies on their hips much of the time are impeding their children's growth and development. From the earliest stages in infancy, place your child on a blanket on the floor or in a "playpen." Let her move, wiggle, roll, stretch, and reach.

Provide a diet rich in variety. Make regular visits to health care providers like doctors and dentists, and follow their advice. Show all family members love and respect. Work at a system of open communication in your home with clear rules and expectations. Establish a family mealtime.

It is also vital that you monitor your child's diet. Consult with your pediatrician about the frequency of meals, the amounts of food, and the nutritional balance needed for optimum growth. Intake of fatty foods and sugar should be monitored and kept at a minimum.

The activities below link directly to the items in the checklist. If your child has scored "low" in a particular area of growing where you think she should do better, study the activity in the list below and incorporate it into your child's routine. Feel free to adapt or expand the activity to suit your home and situation. Most of all, have fun with these activities, and make your child aware of how she is growing and how wonderful it feels to be healthy! Although these activities are designed to practice and reinforce specific aspects of growth, they cannot be successful until they're brought to life; only you can make the teaching and learning process fun.

0-4 Months

Gaining Weight

Avoid strict eating and sleeping schedules but keep a regular routine—the same activities in the same order around the same times. Check with your health care provider about proper nutrition and nighttime feeding recommendations.

Make feedings pleasurable by being prepared before your baby gets frantically hungry. Feed your baby in a relaxed manner, taking the time to talk to her while she eats.

Keep records of your baby's weight as measured during doctor appointments, and note weight gains.

Getting Longer

Keep track of your baby's measurements in length as recorded during doctor visits.

Lay your baby on her stomach and hold and move an enticing toy all around her, causing her to move and lift her head.

Hearing Normally

Check your baby's hearing by talking to her when she is alert and when it is quiet. If she responds by looking at you, moving, smiling, or frowning she is probably hearing your voice.

Getting Vaccinations

Talk with your health care provider to be sure your baby has had all the vaccinations and preventive tests and treatments important to her physical development.

Be sure your baby gets two of three DTP and polio vaccinations. DTP stands for diphtheria, tetanus, and pertussis and is usually administered in one vaccination. Your health care provider will have a specific schedule for your baby and may recommend additional tests and immunizations.

Sleeping 11 to 18 Hours

Keep a regular routine of a morning and afternoon nap with a nighttime stretch of 8 to 14 hours each day for your baby. Your baby may have her own personal schedule but probably needs a total of 11 to 18 hours of sleep per 24-hour period.

Start your bedtime routine about the same time each evening. Follow a predictable, regular bedtime routine that relaxes and comforts your baby, like reading the same book, feeding her a bottle, singing her the same song, rocking her the same way, then putting her to bed firmly in the same way.

Provide a quiet, calm environment for your baby to relax and settle down in before expecting her to fall asleep.

Help your baby be ready for sleep by providing periods of play and activity each day. Play with your baby actively and encourage her to move her arms, legs, and head many times each day. Engage her by making eye contact and touching her face, arms, hands, legs, and feet and playfully and gently moving them around. This will stimulate her appetite and encourage her to eat and sleep well and will result in healthy growth.

5-8 Months

Gaining Weight

Keep track of your baby's weight as measured during doctor visits. Your baby should be gaining weight proportionate to her length and based upon her previous weight.

Stand your baby up against upholstered furniture, supporting and protecting her from falls. Help her shift her weight from one foot to the other by gently rocking her from side to side. This is a good time to sing little songs or repeat little rhymes.

Getting Longer

Keep track of your baby's length as measured during doctor visits. Your baby should be growing in length proportionate to her weight gain and based upon her previous length.

Encourage your baby to reach and stretch. Place your baby near a low padded couch, chair, or sturdy stool and put a favored toy on the furniture within your baby's range of vision. Shake the toy and talk to your baby, saying things like "Come get the toy," or "What is your toy doing up here, can you get it back?" Praise and reward her efforts by giving her the toy or standing her up to get it.

Getting Vaccinations

Arrange for your baby's vaccinations. Local public health departments usually provide low or no-cost immunizations. Your baby should now have her third and final DTP vaccination. Your health care provider will have a specific schedule for your child and may recommend additional tests and immunizations. Keep track of vaccinations and immunizations in a baby book.

Cutting Teeth

Your baby should have two to four teeth at this age. Her first tooth will probably be one of the bottom front teeth. Provide your baby with a teething ring, cold rag for sucking, and teething foods to help her cut her teeth through.

Sleeping

Your baby should now sleep a total of 9 to 18 hours. She should start to sleep 8 to 13 hours at night with two naps during the day per 24-hour period.

Put your baby to bed after your regular calming routine while she is still awake. This will help her to learn how to fall asleep without you. Use motor activities during the day that encourage active play for sleeping.

9-12 Months

Gaining Weight

Check your baby's weight during your regular doctor's visit or weigh her at home. Her weight should be from 17 to 27 pounds for most babies this age.

Your baby should be gaining weight proportionate to her length and based upon her previous weight. Stimulate your baby's growth by playing actively with her.

Getting Longer

Most babies at this age are measuring 27 to 32 inches long. Your baby should be growing in length proportionate to her weight gain and based upon her previous length. Your baby will grow longer with plenty of sleep, daytime activity and proper nutrition.

Teething

Check your baby's teeth. She should now have from five to seven teeth. She probably has all four of her front teeth by now. Use a "finger" brush (a rubber bristled finger sleeve) and rub your baby's teeth and gums while you sing her a song.

Getting Vaccinations

Be sure your baby is given her tuberculin and hematocrit or hemoglobin tests. Your health care provider will have a specific schedule for your baby and may recommend additional tests and immunizations. Keep a calendar and mark well ahead when to schedule doctor appointments.

Hearing

Your baby should be hearing well. Check to see that she responds to a voice in a quiet setting. In a quiet room and from behind your baby, say something she is sure to respond to, like "Do you want a cookie?" If she responds, her hearing is satisfactory. Testing your baby's hearing too often could desensitize her and she will stop responding.

13-16 Months

Gaining Weight

At this age, most babies are weighing from 17 to 29 pounds—something you should be checking periodically. She should be gaining weight proportionate to her length and based upon her previous weight.

Plenty of love and affection will help your baby feel emotionally stable, ensure good sleep and appetite, and allow her to grow physically.

Getting Taller

Most babies should now measure 27 to 33 inches tall. Your baby should continue to grow in height proportionate to her weight gain and based upon her previous height.

Teething

Check to see that your baby has eight to ten teeth. She should continue to cut teeth and at this milestone should have all eight (four on top and four on the bottom) of her front teeth.

Take your baby with you when you brush your teeth and make silly faces in the mirror while brushing. Give her own toothbrush.

Getting Vaccinations

Be sure your baby is given measles, mumps, and rubella vaccinations. Health care providers frequently refer to these as MMRs and will have a specific schedule for your baby. Ask for the first appointment in the morning if you seem to wait a lot for your doctor.

Sleeping

Check to see that your baby sleeps a total of 9 to 12 hours. Your baby's sleep requirements should be lessening, leaving her more time to play and learn.

Encourage active, physical play to promote good sleeping patterns.

17-20 Months

Gaining Weight

At your next doctor's appointment, check to see if your toddler weighs from 18 to 32 pounds. She should be gaining weight proportionate to her height and based upon her previous weight

Encourage active play to stimulate your toddler's appetite.

Getting Taller

Measure your toddler's height—she should be 29 to 36 inches tall. There are fun and attractive "growth charts" that you can put up on a wall in your toddler's room. Make your own family growth chart using a yardstick attached to a wall. Use the chart to track your toddler's growing height as she get older.

Show her the chart and point out what a big girl she is. Your toddler should be growing in height proportionate to her weight gain and based upon her previous height.

Teething

Your toddler should now have 11 to 15 teeth. By this milestone, your toddler should have a molar or two. Let your toddler brush her teeth while you read her stories, or while she watches TV or listens to a tape.

Getting Vaccinations

Schedule a doctor visit for your toddler to get the DTP booster and final polio vaccination. Your health care provider will have a specific schedule for your toddler and may recommend additional tests and immunizations. Some health care providers recommend a dose of children's non-aspirin pain reliever (never aspirin) one-half hour before shots to reduce side effects—ask your pediatrician about this.

Hearing

Always be aware of your toddler's hearing ability. Check to see if she responds to a voice in a quiet setting. In a quiet room and from behind your toddler, say something she is sure to respond to, like "You must go to bed." If she responds, her hearing is satisfactory.

Test your toddler's hearing when she is feeling well and is alert. Colds, allergy symptoms and ear and throat infections may interfere with your toddler's hearing ability.

21-24 Months

Gaining Weight

Your toddler now should weigh between 21 and 33 pounds. She should continue to gain weight proportionate to her height and based upon her previous weight. Be sure to continue to monitor her eating and see that she is eating well to promote growth. Your health care provider can give you guidelines about your toddler's nutritional needs.

Getting Taller

Use your toddler's growth chart to see if she measures 31 to 37 inches tall. She should continue to grow in height proportionate to her weight gain and based upon her previous height. A fun way to track your toddler's growth is to have her lie on a large sheet of paper or newsprint taped together. Trace the outline of her body, cut it out, put it up on the wall, and measure it.

Teething

Check to see if your toddler has 16 to 18 teeth. She should have all eight front teeth, four molars, and some cuspids (eye teeth).

Encourage your toddler to brush longer by counting while she brushes. Can she brush until you count to 10, or during a whole song you sing?

Getting Vaccinations

Be sure your toddler gets her Hib (*Haemophilus influenzae* type B) immunization. Your health care provider will have a specific schedule for your toddler and may recommend additional tests and immunizations. Sometimes the last appointment of the day is a good one because your doctor and staff will be striving to finish on time.

Sleeping

Your toddler should be sleeping a total of 9 to 12 hours. You may still put your toddler down for an afternoon nap, and the remainder of needed sleep will occur at night. Once your toddler is put to bed for the night, allow her three "tickets" for getting out of bed. She may use a ticket to get up for drinks, potty, or to kiss and hug you. Once the tickets are gone, do not allow any more getting up.

25-30 Months

Gaining Weight

Your toddler should weigh 22 to 35 pounds, and should be gaining weight proportionate to her height and based upon her previous weight. Continue to provide her with nutritionally sound meals to help her grow. Bring your toddler grocery shopping and let her choose a fruit or vegetable to try.

Getting Taller

Measure your toddler's height to see if she is between 32 and 39 inches tall. She should be continuing to grow in height proportionate to her weight gain and based upon her previous height. Your toddler's physical growth will be enhanced when she participates in the moving, communicating, relating, thinking, and adapting activities described in this book.

Staying Dry

Notice whether your toddler has a dry diaper after napping. This may be your first indication that your toddler's urination and bowel movements are becoming voluntary and can be controlled by her. Notice whether she is able to hold her urine for up to 1 hour. Draw attention to your toddler's dry diapers by saying things like "Look, your diaper is dry!"

Take your toddler to the bathroom with you and let her turn on the light, watch, get the toilet paper, flush, and wash her hands with you.

Teething

Check to see if your toddler has 18 to 20 teeth. Her teeth should include all eight front teeth, four to eight molars, and one to four cuspids or eye teeth.

Practice rinsing and spitting by showing your toddler how to hold water in your puffed cheeks, then spit into the sink. Let her play and practice to her heart's content.

Hearing

Note whether your toddler hears well and responds to directions. Give your toddler a few easy directions that are fun and rewarding, like "Run to the post and back" or "Go get yourself a treat." If she responds, even to refuse or argue, she shows that she is hearing you.

Practice simple directions like "Stop," "Run," and "Bring me the book." Then use those directions to check your toddler's hearing. Be sure she is feeling cooperative and that the directions are not new to her.

31-36 Months

Gaining Weight

Your growing toddler now weighs 24 to 38 pounds. She continues to gain weight proportionate to her height and based upon her previous weight.

Monitor your toddler's nutritional intake. Serve a variety of foods. Let your preschooler choose at least three items to start, then more after she has tried her first three.

Getting Taller

Your toddler should now measure 34 to 41 inches tall, growing in height proportionate to her weight gain and based upon her previous height. Spend plenty of time outdoors, in gymnasiums, and on playgrounds, chasing balls, flying kites, playing tag, and going for walks during all seasons. All of these physical activities will encourage your toddler's growth.

Teething

Check to see if your toddler has 20 teeth, marking the completion of her first teeth.

Use an audio recording, a song, or a TV commercial and see if your toddler can brush the whole time.

Sleeping

Your toddler should be sleeping a total of 9 to 12 hours. She may need an afternoon nap, but most sleep occurs at night. A good consequence for breaking bedtime rules is "no story" or "no song."

Going to the Dentist

Schedule your toddler's first dental examination. Most dentists recommend that your toddler's first dental exam occur after she has all 20 of her baby teeth, then regularly and at least yearly thereafter.

Play dentist with your preschooler. Go to her door and say something like "The dentist will see you now," sit on the couch with her head on your lap, and do some of the things a dentist and hygienist would do. End with brushing and flossing her teeth gently.

37-42 Months

Gaining Weight

Your preschooler should weigh from 25 to 40 pounds. She should be gaining weight proportionate to her height and based upon her previous weight.

Getting Taller

Measure your preschooler's height using her growth chart. She should stand 35 to 42 inches tall. She should be growing in height proportionate to her weight gain and based upon her previous height. Farmer's markets and roadside produce stands are wonderful for sampling fruits and vegetables, looking at colors, and talking about growing things.

Losing the Toddler Look

Stand back and look at your preschooler and compare how she looks now to how she looked 6 to 12 months ago. You should notice that her legs have lengthened and her stomach has flattened. Your child looks a little leaner and has a straighter posture by this milestone. You should notice that her pants are getting too short, even though they may fit around the waist. Your preschooler will delight in comparing her height to that of others. Encourage her to stand next to you to see how high she comes on you.

Hearing

Observe whether your preschooler hears well—whether she responds to a whisper. In a quiet room and from behind her, whisper something she is sure to respond to, like "Do you want a cookie?" If she responds, her hearing is good. If you sense problems, schedule a formal evaluation with your doctor's office. Try some of the communication activities that involve whispering.

Public school systems may be able to help you with early screening for hearing

Eyesight

Check to see that your preschooler sees well. Assuming that you have good (even if lens-corrected) vision, check whether your preschooler is able to see things that you can see at varying distances. You may want to have her vision checked at your doctor's office to be certain her eyesight is okay. Your public school system may be able to help with early vision screening.

43-48 Months

Gaining Weight

Your preschooler should weigh from 27 to 43 pounds, gaining weight proportionate to her height and based upon her previous weight. Ensure that she is eating a nutritionally balanced diet, following your health care provider's guidelines. Use a magazine with photos of good foods. Let your preschooler cut out pictures to create her own grocery list. Require her to find pictures of dairy products, grains, and all food groups. Have her take the list to the store with her when you go shopping.

Getting Taller

Check your preschooler's height on her growth chart. She should measures from 36 to 44 inches tall, growing in height proportionate to her weight gain and based upon her previous height. Purchase a dressmaker's tape measure for your preschooler and mark her measurements on the tape. Measure her head, her arms, and her shoulders in addition to her height.

Napping

At this age, your preschooler naps briefly or not at all. It's a good idea to provide your child with a quiet rest period, and not necessarily a nap. Require a rest or a quiet or silent time at the same time each day. Make it a special time to watch a special show or video, to look through books used only during that time, or to listen to audio tapes or radio programs. You may notice that she will nap one day and not the next or nap only briefly.

Sleeping

Schedule your preschooler's bedtime so that she sleeps a total of 9 to 12 hours.

To keep bedtime from becoming an ordeal, establish reasonable rules and a sensible routine with consequences. Talk to your preschooler about those rules each morning. Explain what will happen if rules or routines are broken. Write the rules down. Remind her of the rules at dinnertime and enforce them at bedtime.

Taking Shape

Take a look at your preschooler from a distance. Note whether she has the proportions of a child rather than a toddler. She should appear leaner, with her head and body proportions more like that of a miniature adult. Use movement activities to help your preschooler develop the proportions of a child. Take photos of your preschooler in a swimsuit or shorts and tee shirt. Compare them to photos taken months before.

49-60 Months

Gaining Weight

Your preschooler probably weighs 30 to 50 pounds, and is gaining weight proportionate to her height and based upon her previous weight. Serve only very small portions of foods. Start a little vegetable garden or windowsill garden and help your preschooler grow carrots, peas, tomatoes, or a favorite food.

Getting Taller

When you measure your preschooler's height, you may find that she is 38 to 46 inches tall and is gaining height proportionate to her weight and based upon her previous height. Do the stretch. Using something you store in a high place, let your preschooler stretch to get it and note how far she can reach.

Getting Vaccinations

Be sure your preschooler has had DTP and polio booster shots. Your health care provider will have a specific schedule for your child and may recommend additional tests and immunizations.

Before each exam, play doctor and nurse with your preschooler, instructing her about shots, medicines, and eye, ear, nose, and throat inspections.

Hearing Screening

Schedule a hearing screening for your preschooler. Hearing screenings are usually done during the child's first year in school—ask for the results. Call your local public school system or state public health department and take advantage of preschool kindergarten screenings for vision and hearing. Ask your preschooler to mimic your tones and words. Sit behind her and say various words at different pitches and degrees of loudness, noting which sounds she misses. Share this information with your pediatrician.

Vision Screening

Schedule a vision test and see how your preschooler responds to an "E" chart eye test. This is a vision screening test, the first formal vision test your child may have. It is usually given during the child's first year in school—ask for the results. Take a picture or look through old photos of your preschooler taken from straight ahead with eyes on the camera. Look closely at the photo. Is an equal amount of white showing in both eyes? If not, one eye may have weak muscles, so consult with your pediatrician.

61-72 Months

Gaining Weight

Weigh your child—she should weigh 33 to 57 pounds, and should be gaining weight proportionate to her height and based upon her previous weight. Be sure she is active during the day, and eats well-balanced, nutritional meals to stimulate growth. Employ your child's help in food preparations and meal planning. This can be one of her chores and a regularly scheduled activity.

Getting Taller

Check your preschooler's height—she should measure 42 to 49 inches tall. She should grow in height proportionate to her weight gain and based upon her previous height. Growth in height at this age will slow, so increases will be in fractions of inches. Be sure you are measuring the same way each time.

Healthy Feet and Legs

Look at your preschooler's feet to see whether they have arches and her legs are straight. While your child may not develop arches because of heredity, if she is going to, it will happen now. Her legs should have lost most of their bowing, although a little "toeing in" is normal and will not cause a problem. If you notice an abnormality or have questions, discuss your concerns with your health care provider.

Encourage your child to be active in running and jumping to build strong muscles which help her to sit, stand, play, run, and jump with good posture.

Fewer Colds and Flu

Take note as to whether your preschooler has fewer colds and flu. She should be building up immunities to colds and flu with increased exposure to larger groups of children. Encourage frequent hand washing during the cold season along with the careful practice of not sharing drinking glasses, straws, spoons, tissues, and toothbrushes.

Scoliosis Screening

Schedule a scoliosis/posture screening for your preschooler. This is usually a routine screening test your health care provider or school personnel will perform—ask for the results.

Appendix

Milestone Descriptions

Moving

0-4 Months

Holds head up for 10 or more seconds. While held on your shoulder or seated on your lap, your child holds her head up and steady for a slow count to ten.

Reaches and grabs a toy. In passing this milestone your child reaches or swipes, however inaccurately, and grabs a toy.

Rolls over. Your child rolls from side to side, front to back, or back to front.

Sits steadily when held. You can also seat your child surrounded by pillows or in a baby seat to evaluate her ability to sit without slumping.

Pushes up on arms. While lying on her stomach, your child pushes against the surface, straightening her arms and lifting up her head and chest completely.

5-8 Months

Creeps, crawls, or otherwise moves about. Your child moves purposefully to things she wants — she may be a sophisticated roller, tummy crawler, scooter, or have a truly unique way of getting around.

Passes a toy from one hand to the other. Your child begins to use her hands by passing things from one hand to the other without dropping them.

Pulls self to standing. Your child may pull up holding on to your fingers, furniture, or anything else. Also consider this step as complete if your child stands up without help.

Picks up small toys with fingertips. Using the pads of her fingers and thumb, as opposed to using her whole hand or palm, your child picks up small toys or pieces of food.

Makes walking motion when held. Your child walks forward, bearing weight on alternating feet when you hold her by the hand(s) or under her arms.

9-12 Months

Creeps or crawls up two or more steps. Check this milestone as complete if your child moves up two or more steps by any means or in any manner. Be sure you are nearby and have provided a safe environment for your child to practice this skill.

Walks, holding on to furniture. Frequently called cruising, your child walks along furniture holding on for support and for balance.

Picks up and puts down small toys. Watch your child pick up and intentionally put down a toy.

Stands alone. Your child lets go of support, often intentionally, and stands for a few seconds or more unsupported. It doesn't matter how your child gets to a standing position.

Sits down from standing. Consider this step accomplished if your child lowers herself with control to either a sitting, crawling, or lying position.

13-16 Months

Bends or stoops and stands again. The point of this item is to evaluate your child's balance while moving. To achieve this step, your child will be able to stand unsupported, then bend or stoop (usually to pick something up) and stand again without falling.

Puts small toys into a container. Watch for your child's intentional and accurate placement of objects into a container, like putting a block into a dump truck, or a ball into a box.

Hurls or throws objects. Your child may delight in energetically throwing things with no particular target in mind.

Walks well. Your child walks confidently, starting and stopping easily without falling.

Walks backward or sideways. Your child takes several steps backward or sideways on her own.

17-20 Months

Walks while pushing, pulling, or carrying. You notice your child's skill in pushing, pulling, or carrying objects while walking.

Imitates simple motions. Your child enjoys copying your simple movements, like circling arms, kicking, head-shaking, and bending over.

Climbs up and down furniture. Your child gets on and off adult-sized furniture without help.

Stands on one foot holding on. You might notice this skill during shoe-tying or dressing. Can your child lift one foot up while she holds on to you or something sturdy so that you can tie her shoe? Can she stand and step into pants while holding on?

Walks, picks up a toy, and walks again. This item evaluates your child's walking and balancing as she is able to walk, stoop to pick up an object, and then continue walking again.

21-24 Months

Jumps down from a low step. Your child jumps from a low step with both feet together at the same time.

Kicks a ball. Your child momentarily balances on one leg while swinging the other to kick an object.

Runs forward. Your child runs in a general forward direction without falling.

Stands up easily. At this milestone, your child smoothly stands up from a sitting position.

Throws a ball overhand. Watch as your child throws a ball forward with her hand passing over her shoulder.

25-30 Months

Walks up and down stairs alone. Your child may use a handrail or wall for support, but walks up and down stairs without your help, even if she puts both feet on a step.

Jumps in place two or more times. Your child jumps up and down with feet landing at the same time.

Runs or walks on tiptoe. This item is intended to evaluate your child's ability to do more difficult balancing while moving. Running on tiptoe is easier than walking.

Climbs on a jungle gym. With supervised safe climbing, your child passes this milestone if she can climb on basic playground equipment.

Walks backward 10 or more feet. If you watch your child play, she will probably walk backward to pull toys, arrange things, or to move out of the way.

31-36 Months

Jumps forward with feet together. Both feet leave the ground together and land forward of where your child started.

Stands on one foot for 2 or more seconds. In this item your child stands unsupported, on either foot for the slow count of two, showing standing balance.

Steers and pedals a tricycle. When your child is ready, it takes only a few days of practice on a tricycle to pass this milestone.

Throws a ball underhand. Your child finds success with this item using a small (tennis size) ball or a bean bag. In underhand throwing your child's hand swings below her shoulder past her hip and she releases the ball in a forward direction.

Walks upstairs one foot on each step. To consider this step accomplished, your child should be able to go upstairs without using a handrail or wall for support.

37-42 Months

Walks downstairs one foot on each step. Your child passes this milestone if she descends steps, one foot on each step, without using a handrail, a wall, or someone's hand for support.

Catches a large ball. Your child can catch a ball in any manner to pass this milestone.

Runs around obstacles. Your child runs close to things without running into them, turning corners easily.

Hops in place on one foot. Watch your child as she hops in place on one foot two or more times, keeping her balance.

Walks on a straight line or curb. Moving balance is important for future movement skills. Encourage your child to walk on lines, cracks in the pavement, safe curbs, or low walls (with supervision).

43-48 Months

Hops forward on one foot two or more hops. Your child's moving balance continues to develop, making it possible for her to hop a short distance with purpose and control.

Catches a large bounced ball. Toss a ball so that it bounces in front of your child. Watch as she catches it with one or both arms.

Gallops. Your child skips on one foot, with the same foot always leading.

Walks forward heel touching toe. Watch as your child walks in a straight line heel-to-toe, keeping her balance.

Jumps over an object with both feet. Place a shoestring, tissue, or stick on the floor and tell your child to jump over it. Watch as your child jumps over the object without touching it, landing on both feet at the same time.

49-60 Months

Catches a ball with hands. As your child's coordination improves, she catches a ball with her hands, relying less on her chest or arms to "trap" the ball.

Balances on tiptoes for 10 or more seconds. Your child stands on her tiptoes and keeps her balance for at least 10 seconds.

Jumps over knee-high obstacles. With greater strength and agility, your child jumps with both feet over higher objects without touching them (such as a loosely held jump rope).

Walks backward toe touching heel. Your child walks backward toe-to-heel, keeping her balance.

Hops forward on one foot six or more hops. Your child uses her arms to help her hop in a controlled manner.

61-72 Months

Skips. As your child skips, she is alternating forward hops on each foot.

Touches toes without bending knees. From a standing position, your child bends at her waist and touches her toes, showing flexibility.

Rides a two-wheel bike. Your child starts, steers, and stops a two-wheel bike without falling.

Bounces and catches a ball with one hand. Allow your child to use her preferred hand to bounce and catch a tennis-sized ball.

Balances on one foot for 10 or more seconds. Your child stands on one foot with little arm or trunk movement for a slow count to 10.

Communicating

0-4 Months

Coos and babbles. The first sounds, besides crying, that your child intentionally makes are coos and babbles.

Makes a vowel sound. Your child makes any of the vowel sounds (a, e, i, o, and u). Sounds may include ah, oh, uh, and so forth.

Laughs out loud. Whether in response to you or on her own, you hear your child laugh.

Responds to a voice. Your child's responses might include quieting, listening, turning her head, opening her eyes, or awakening to the sound of a familiar voice in a quiet room.

Makes sounds for attention. You may be surprised to hear your child clicking her tongue, cooing, babbling, or gurgling, in addition to her crying to get attention.

5-8 Months

Makes three or more sounds in one breath. Sounds can be like "ba-ba-ba," or "da-ba-ka."

Says at least two different sounds like "da" and "ba." These don't have to be successive or in the same breath, just any two different syllables. "Ka," "ma," and "mu" are common sounds children make at this age.

Makes sounds of at least two syllables. The syllable sounds your child makes don't need to be the same — she may say "da-ba," or "da-ba-ka," or "da-da-da," and she would still pass this milestone. The point of this item is that the sounds are made successively.

Responds to own name. Looking, listening, smiling, and quieting are ways your child might respond when you say her name.

Shouts. Your child may not use intelligible words, but she definitely knows how to holler for attention when she reaches this step.

9-12 Months

Imitates sounds. At this stage your child tries to copy the sounds you make.

Listens to familiar words. Your sometimes distracted or inattentive child will begin to pay attention to words she hears you say frequently.

Says "no" and shakes head. This milestone shows that your child understands the word "no."

Says two or more words clearly to the parent. Don't be concerned if no one else understands what your child is saying as long as you do.

Uses Mama or Dada as names. This milestone means that your child has names (like Mama or Dada or others) and uses them for the key people in her household.

13-16 Months

Says four or more words clearly to others. Until now, no one but you were able to understand your child's speech.

Follows simple directions. Some good simple directions to try might include "Bring me the ___," "Take a cookie," and "Sit in your chair." Try these or other simple commands to see if your child listens, understands, and responds.

Uses at least one word to express an idea. For example, your child may say "eat," and, depending upon the context, it means "I want to eat" or "Are we eating?" or "Those people are eating."

Asks for things by name. Your child uses one key word, like "cookie," "bottle," or "ball," to show what she wants.

Makes up own meaningful words. Your child will have specific meaningful words that are not real words. These words may be names for family members, names of familiar items, or greetings.

17-20 Months

Listens to music or stories for 3 or more minutes. In a quiet room, read a story or play an audio recording that your child chooses to note her attention span.

Uses 10 or more different words. You might enjoy making an audio recording or making a list of the words your child uses at this stage.

Babbles or talks into a play phone. Your child makes "pretend" conversation with a play phone.

Answers simple questions. Your child answers questions like "Do you want a drink?" or "Where is Mommy?" or "What do you want to eat?"

Names most familiar objects. Your child will be able to name almost everything (90 percent, or nine out of ten things) familiar to her.

21-24 Months

Uses 20 or more words. Your child uses at least 20 different words during her daily "conversation."

Answers "What is your name?" Your child will be able to tell others her first name at this milestone.

Imitates new words. As you say new words, your child enjoys copying them. This step of development introduces your child to more and more words.

Repeats at least one line of a rhyme. A line from any Mother Goose rhyme, a rhyme that you make up, or one taken from a song can make good rhymes to repeat. Say or sing the rhyme and then ask your child to say it.

Uses at least two words together. Simple two-word sentences mark this step. Your child uses two words to communicate an idea, like "Go bye-bye," or "Daddy home."

25-30 Months

Imitates parent's tone of voice. You are sure to see a reflection of yourself when your child takes this step. She uses her voice as you do when you answer the phone, scold her, greet others, or ask questions.

Repeats parts of songs and rhymes. Your child will correctly repeat more than two lines of a song or rhyme.

Uses sentences of at least three words. When your child consistently uses three or more words in a sentence to express herself, she is well on her way to being an efficient communicator.

Uses personal pronouns I, you, me. Your child approaches this step when she starts referring to herself as "me," as in "Me want cookie." When she uses I, you, and me correctly, she has completely passed this milestone.

Asks questions. You may tire of your child's endless questions during this stage.

31-36 Months

Takes part in a conversation. Conversations may be brief, but they follow a logical pattern. They are clearly a verbal give-and-take.

Answers "who, where, and when" questions. Your child clearly answers questions like "Who did that?" "Where are you going?" and "When did it happen?"

Adds many new words each month. During this period, your child is adding about 50 new words each month. Although you may not be able to keep track of the number of new words your child is using each month, you notice an amazing variety of new expressions your child uses.

Tells what to do when hungry, thirsty, sleepy, etc. Ask your child, "What do you do when you are thirsty?" (and similar questions) and listen for her correct answers.

Uses in, on, empty, and full. You will notice mastery of this step when your child correctly uses these words to describe the relationship among objects.

37-42 Months

Talks clearly. By this step your child says most words clearly enough for you and everyone else to understand.

Tells what is happening in pictures. Show your child snapshots, magazine pictures, or pictures in a book and ask her what is happening. She has passed this milestone when she appropriately tells you what is going on in the picture.

Uses plurals. While your child may not be proficient at irregular plurals (saying "mouses" instead of "mice"), she adds the "s" ending to words to indicate more than one (like horses).

Uses *the* and *a*. The sentences your child makes include *the* and *a* and her sentences sound more correct.

Knows all the words to a song or rhyme. The words to a song like "London Bridge," "Rock-a-Bye Baby," "Happy Birthday," or rhymes like "Humpty-Dumpty," "Rain, Rain, Go Away," and "Hickory Dickory Dock," come easily to your child at this stage.

43-48 Months

Talks about imaginary situations. "Mom, if we had a swimming pool, I would climb up on the roof and jump in," is an example of how your child might talk when she reaches this stage.

Listens to stories for 20 minutes or longer. In a quiet room, let your child choose a book for you to read or an audio recording to play for at least 20 minutes to note her attention span.

Plays with words; makes up new words. Word play shows your child's developing understanding of language. "Dad, that's a tork, not a fork," or "Grandma, I want a chocanookie," or "Mom, it's so big, it's huge-a-tiffic," are examples of ways your child might make up new words.

Uses four or five words for feelings. Sad, happy, angry, excited, and frustrated are some feeling words your child might use. She may likely use the feeling words she hears from you, so use a variety!

Laughs at and uses silly rhyming. Try changing the words to a familiar holiday song onto a silly rhyme, like "Jingle bells, Batman smells, Robin laid an egg." Your child should laugh and delight at the sound and try some of her own. The words might make little or no sense and the phrases be ridiculous, but your child shows continued interest in what she can do with language.

49-60 Months

Clearly says own first and last names. To communicate with others outside her family, she pronounces her entire name clearly, and may begin to correct mispronunciations. This step is important for her safety outside the home.

Can argue with words. Words begin to replace actions as your child learns to assert herself using words instead of physical outbursts.

Uses jokes and silly language. The jokes may not be funny to others, but your child will be pleased with them. For example, "Knock, knock. Who's there? Underwear."

Uses sentences of at least five words. At this milestone, your child uses fairly lengthy sentences of five or six words — maybe even more.

Makes "b, p, m, w, h, d, t, n, g, k, ng, y" sounds. These sounds may fall anywhere in the word. Good words to try are: bug, put, mom, we, have, dog, cat, song, and yes.

61-72 Months

Gives full name, age, and address. Your child will need to recite this information correctly for school and for personal safety.

Talks about own feelings. Ask short simple questions to encourage your child to talk about her feelings — for example, "How did that make you feel?" Listen for answers of two to three sentences or longer.

Identifies the first sound in words. Your child says things like "snake begins with ssss." While she may not be able to identify the letter as "s," she does pass this milestone.

Uses well-constructed sentences. Your child uses nouns and verb tenses correctly. Her sentences will usually follow traditional rules of grammar, showing emerging sophistication with language — her sentences sound correct.

Shares experiences with others. Watch your child's success at "show and tell," or in other situations where she describes with some detail her recent activities.

Relating

0-4 Months

Shows excitement. Your child may show her excitement by stiffening, quieting, and arm flailing. Regardless of how she shows she is excited, you will certainly know when she is!

Makes sounds or moves to get attention. Each time you give attention to your child's movements and sounds, it encourages her to repeat the action. Note whether, after you give her attention, she repeats the movement or sound.

Shows interest in mirror image. Hold your child so that she is facing a mirror. Note whether she shows interest by intently staring, smiling, reaching toward it, or suddenly quieting from crying.

Plays with own hands. Your child brings her hands together so that one touches or grabs the other and she intently watches her hands as she manipulates them together.

Smiles and laughs when talked to. Talk to your child and watch her reaction. This is an exciting milestone because it shows that your child is aware of you and responds to your attention. This relationship forms the model upon which all other relationships are built.

5-8 Months

Smiles and laughs at baby games. Play games with your child like "peek-a-boo," "this little piggy," "so big," and "where's the baby," and watch to see if she enjoys them.

Wants parents and siblings over strangers. While your child may not yet cry or fuss around strangers, she will certainly act happier and be more contented when held by you or other well-known family members.

Cries when separated from parent. Separation anxiety is an important milestone for your child. If your child cries when you separate from her, it shows that she has a strong bond with you — an important step at this age.

Touches or smiles at mirror image. Your child may be "in love" with her mirror image. She may try to "kiss" or otherwise touch that beautiful baby in the mirror.

Shows pleasure and displeasure. At this stage your child has definite preferences and she is eager to express herself. Pleasure might be shown by smiling, cooing, or laughing, whereas displeasure may be shown with a quick bat at the object or person followed by cries, stiffening, or kicking.

9-12 Months

Shows moods by looking hurt, happy, or sad. Watch your child and note whether she expresses her moods and feelings — an important phase in emotional development.

Plays with adults or older children. Your child initiates and takes part in various forms of play, first with adults and older children. Play may include examining toys, dancing to music, or dropping toys for others to pick up among other games.

Plays "pat-a-cake," "peek-a-boo," and "so-big." Earlier, your child laughed at and smiled at these baby games; now, she imitates and actively takes part in them.

Offers toys to others. Your child offers, even hands toys to others, but may not actually let go of them.

Seeks approval and responds to "no." At this stage your child wants to please you. She stops an action when told "No," not to do it, is unhappy when you are unhappy with something she has done, and tries to do things to please you.

13-16 Months

Smiles easily and shows affection for others. Your child hugs, kisses, and snuggles to show her affection.

Gives a toy without wanting it back immediately. Now your developing child is able to actually give up a toy or other item. She may want to check if she will get it back, but is willing to give it up for a short period of time.

Enjoys being around children. You will notice that your child gets excited or is more content when she is around other children.

Plays chase me/catch me games. Unsophisticated versions of tag delight your child at this milestone and she may want to play these games repeatedly.

Expresses many emotions. Now your child shows emotions beyond happiness, sadness, anger, and frustration — she may show excitement, joy, apprehension, anxiety, delight, and puzzlement.

17-20 Months

Demands the company of others. Passing this milestone shows that your child insists that others play with her or be with her.

Enjoys rough-house play with parent. Wrestling, tickling, and being tossed around, are all activities in which your child delights.

Spends time looking at self in mirror. Your child spends time (a few minutes or more) just looking or even talking to herself in the mirror. This item measures your child's regard for herself — she is gathering information that contributes to her self-concept.

Helps others. However unhelpful it may be, your child wants to "help" others in household chores or other tasks. Acceptance, even encouragement of this "help" contributes to her self-concept and ability to relate to others.

Shows off. Your child may play "shy," then act silly, aggressive, or otherwise perform to get the attention of others.

21-24 Months

Talks to self or to toys when playing. Your child is taking a step toward relating to others by carrying on conversations with herself or her toys during play.

Plays alone in the company of other children. Frequently referred to as "parallel play," when the child plays contentedly alone although there are other children in the room, this behavior marks a step toward play relationships with children.

Shares attention. Before this milestone, your child claimed your attention and found it very difficult to allow you to talk with or watch anyone else. Now, your child is more patient when your attention is diverted. Note that she is also more willing to share the attention of other children and adults.

Likes to please others. Your child looks for and finds many opportunities to please.

Orders others around. You may find yourself chuckling when your child is in this phase — she will holler at and command people to do as she sees fit.

25-30 Months

Imitates mannerisms of parent. At this stage, your child acts like a miniature of you. You will notice her hold her arms, shake her finger, tilt her head, and so forth, just as you do.

Shows affection for a friend. At this stage the friend is often of the opposite sex.

Tests parent's reaction to "no." Your child may not actually be contrary, but says "no" to see what will happen.

Relates feelings with gestures and words. Your child continues to develop her skills in relating to others by expressing her feelings in greater depth through words and gestures.

Calls others "Baby," "Mommy," and "Daddy." You may mistake this for your child's lack of information or knowledge, but it really shows that your child is aware of her relationship with you and the relationships of others.

31-36 Months

Plays cooperatively with another child. This milestone marks the extension of your child's relationships beyond that of her family, as she shares and interacts with another child during play.

Pretends. Your child pretends to be doing the things she sees you and others do. You'll also see her pretend to be a character from a movie, a video, or a book.

Shows disgust. The emotion of disgust reveals itself at this stage, as certain images, objects, and smells appear very unappealing to your child.

Shows interest in TV. Your child attentively watches certain programs, parts of programs or commercials on TV.

Plays in a group. Your child participates as a member of a group — taking turns and helping others.

37-42 Months

Calls attention to own performance. For example, your child says, "Look at me, look at me," "I made this," or "Watch what I can do" to get your attention for her accomplishments.

Interacts with other children. Now your child relates to other children beyond playing. She discusses plans for play, tells about her experiences, and shows things to other children.

Shows sympathy toward others. Your child may ask, "Are you okay?" or "Oh, that must hurt" to show genuine concern for someone else. She may also offer help and gestures of comfort.

Spends extended time in favorite activities. Your child enjoys spending 20 minutes or more in activities like blowing bubbles, sailing boats, playing with sand, or building blocks, painting, and playing with clay.

Is friendly and agreeable. This stage is marked by your child's spirit of cooperation and happy disposition.

43-48 Months

Shares toys. Your developing child is very willing to share her toys, confident now that she will get them back.

Shows self-control. Watch as your child resists the temptation to touch things in stores or handle forbidden objects. She may even stop herself from whining, crying, or throwing a tantrum.

Takes part in group activities. Your child can actively and appropriately participate in a group activity led by a teacher or supervisor.

Is attached to one friend. At this stage, your child chooses a primary friend, usually of the same sex.

Respects others and their things. You will notice your child showing care when handling things important to other people.

49-60 Months

Prefers same-sex friends. At this stage, boys usually play with other boys and girls prefer to play with other girls.

Enjoys performing for others. Your child asks you to watch as she puts on "plays" and puppet shows, and performs physical feats.

Whispers and has secrets. Your child is able to keep a secret such as the contents of a package or a surprise; she enjoys secrets and likes to whisper to someone else.

Responds to praise and blame. At this stage, your child's feelings are particularly vulnerable even if she doesn't show it. You will see her "shine" when you praise her, and feel "bad" when she is blamed for something.

Prefers other children over adults. Your child has developed to the stage where she would rather be with other children than with you or most other adults. This stage shows that your child is relating to children her own age.

61-72 Months

Shows socially acceptable behavior. This milestone is marked by your child showing an awareness of common rules of etiquette. Your child says "please" and "thank you" without prompting, she uses the table manners you've been demonstrating, and interrupts conversations appropriately.

Follows classroom rules and directions. Your child is especially careful to follow rules at school, even carrying them over at home.

Participates in competitive play. Racing, comparing performances, and winning become important at this stage.

Initiates social contacts. Your child says "Hello" to those she knows, asks other children to play, and shows things to others.

Accepts fair play and fair punishment. Understanding of the concept of fairness, fair play, and fair punishment mark this milestone. You may hear your child protest "that's not fair" at a perceived injustice, and yet, in other circumstances, she accepts fair punishment readily.

Thinking

0-4 Months

Follows moving toy with eyes. Hold an interesting toy at your child's eye level, 8 to 10 inches from her face, and move it slowly in an arc to each side. If she follows the toy with her eyes, she has passed this milestone.

Mouths nearly everything. Your child tries to put everything she can into her mouth. This is important to her investigation of her world; just make it safe by keeping things as clean as possible and too large to choke on.

Turns head and looks toward a sound. Your child uses all of her senses, hearing included, to discover her world. This item shows that your child notices something in her environment.

Touches the facial features of others. Showing early exploration, a child at this stage grabs at, pats, swipes, pokes, and pulls at your nose, eyes, hair, chin, and mouth.

Recognizes family members. You will know that your child recognizes family members because she quiets, excites, kicks, or stiffens when she sees or hears them.

5-8 Months

Watches a toy being hidden and then looks for it. As your child watches, put a toy under a blanket. Even though she may not find the toy, she looks for it with her eyes and reaches for it where it was last seen.

Pulls a string in order to get a toy. This important milestone shows your child's developing thinking skills — she has learned that she can get something she wants by pulling an attached string.

Holds a toy and reaches for another. When your child doesn't drop one toy in order to get another, she recognizes that she can hold on to one and reach for another one.

Explores own body with mouth and hands. Your child pats, grabs, or sucks her fists, wrists, arms, fingers, toes, and even her whole foot as she learns about her body.

Explores by touching, shaking, and tasting objects. At this milestone your child studies objects by manipulating them in every way she can.

9-12 Months

Holds three small toys at the same time. Holding and manipulating many objects shows increased complexity in your child's thinking.

Finds a hidden toy. At this stage your child knows where to look for objects she watches being hidden and knows how to get them. Put a toy she likes under a blanket and watch her uncover it. Hide something small in your fist and she tries to open your fist. Put something she wants in a pocket and she will go after it.

Uses an object as a container for another. Your child has learned an important concept about sizes and shapes of things and how they relate to each other when she puts a spoon into a kettle, a block into a box, or a sock into a hamper.

Imitates actions like scribbling or bell-ringing. Scribble on paper, ring a bell, stir with a spoon, shake a rattle, or clap your hands and your child copies your actions.

Holds a toy and explores with the other hand. Your child uses her hands independently.

13-16 Months

Fits a round piece into a simple puzzle. Using simple three- or five-piece puzzles or formboards, your child fits a simple piece into place correctly.

Turns toys right side up. At this stage, your child recognizes when a toy is upside down and intentionally rights it.

Puts a small object in a bottle and dumps it out. This classic stage is almost always measured by the experts with a raisin and bottle. The bottle's opening is too small for your child to get the raisin out in any other manner but to dump it. This mental concept is learned when your child can put the raisin in the bottle, and importantly, when she turns the bottle over to get it out.

Scribbles with a pencil or crayon. Your child's emerging thinking skills are marked by her spontaneous scribbles with a pencil or crayon.

Points to one or more named body parts. Pointing to and naming body parts are important steps to learning. Your child must first learn about herself before she can learn about other things.

17-20 Months

Knows what to do with a hammer, a phone, etc. Your child shows an understanding of the purpose for certain tools and appliances. Other tools your child may know how to use include tableware, screwdrivers, phones, pliers, and toothbrushes.

Imitates housework. Your child pretends to cook, dust, vacuum, mow the lawn, sew, or wash dishes.

Points to four or more named body parts. Your child points to at least four body parts such as her tummy, foot, knee, hand, finger, ear, or eye.

Puts together a simple two-piece puzzle. The best puzzles for children at this stage are simple shape (triangle, rectangle, square, or circle) puzzles with little knobs on the pieces for ease in placement.

Uses chairs to reach things. Your child also achieves this milestone if she uses sticks or other implements to reach things — the idea is that she has learned how to extend her reach by using an object.

21-24 Months

Makes a circle, a line, or a "V" after watching. Make a circle while your child watches, then ask her to do it. Now do the same with a line, and then a "V." Her copies can be crude approximations to pass this milestone.

Looks for ways to work new toys. When faced with different or new toys at a friend's house, in school, or in waiting areas for children, your child tries to make them "work."

Names four or more pictures. Use pictures of familiar objects and ask your child to name them and note if she can name at least four.

Nests boxes, cups, or stacking rings. Measuring cups or spoons, plastic bowls, rings on a peg, or toys specifically made for nesting are good things for your child to experiment with. Watch to see if she stacks or nests the objects logically.

Puts together a simple three-piece puzzle. Use a simple shape (circle, triangle, or square) puzzle or a very simple puzzle with large pieces to see if your child can place three or more pieces together on her own.

25-30 Months

Waits when told "in a minute," "later," or "pretty soon." Your child waits when hearing one of these or similar phrases, showing a basic understanding about time.

Understands consequences of actions. These consequences and actions might be physical (pulling out a block from a tower results in the tower falling; throwing a rubber ball to the ground will make it bounce, pushing the button on the doorknob will make it lock) as well as behavioral (when I cry, I get things; when I say "thank you," I get praised; when I pick up the toys, I get to go outside).

Builds a six-block tower. Your child builds a tower on her own with blocks, showing mental planning and visual-motor coordination.

Confines scribbles to the page. Your child is gaining some fine motor control as well as an understanding that writing belongs on a piece of paper.

Brings one of something. This milestone marks your child's understanding of the concept of one. Ask your child to bring you one cracker, one puzzle piece, or one block, to see if she truly differentiates one object from more than one.

31-36 Months

Strings three large beads. Be sure to allow your child to use a tipped lace. She picks up the beads one at a time and threads each one onto the string, showing mental planning and visual-motor coordination.

Draws a person (shows head and legs). To pass this stage, your child clearly draws and points out at least the head and legs in her drawing of a person.

Builds with blocks. Your child builds in all directions (up, to each side, and back) to make trains, buildings, towers, and other structures.

Understands in, out, in front of, under, over, etc. You will notice your child's accomplishment in thinking when she follows your directions using these words. Ask her to follow directions like "put the hammer in the cupboard," "take a spoon out of the drawer," "stand in front of the sink," "look under the chair," and "step over the puddle."

Turns pages of a book one-by-one. Your child recognizes the beginning of a book, right-side up, and pages through it one page at a time.

37-42 Months

Differentiates a boy from a girl. Your child recognizes that boys are different from girls and may begin identifying (however inaccurately) certain behaviors and qualities she associates with each.

Counts to 10. Ask your child, with no pictures, objects, or numbers to look at, to count out loud to 10. When she recites the numbers correctly in order, she has passed this milestone.

Identifies two or more familiar objects by touch. This can be a fun game for you and your child. Take favorite toys, household objects, and tools, and one at a time place them in a pillow case or sack without your child watching. Have your child feel the item without looking and try to identify it.

Talks about pictures seen in books. Your child talks about pictures she's seen not only in books, but in magazines, newspapers, on billboards, or on TV. This talk might include questions.

Follows two-step directions. Your child remembers to do at least two things you've told her to do. You might ask her to "brush your teeth, then comb your hair" or "find your shoes, then get your school bag."

43-48 Months

Matches pictures in simple memory games. Lotto games require your child to turn over a card to reveal a picture, then turn it back, but remember where it is when she finds its mate. These games show that she is developing short-term memory.

Points to triangle, circle, rectangle, and square. Draw the shapes on a piece of paper. Your child recognizes and identifies these shapes by pointing to each shape as you say, "Point to the triangle," and so forth.

Remembers recent events. Your child may talk about things she did earlier that day, things she saw the day before, and things she got.

Draws a person (head, trunk, arms, legs, shoulders). When asked to "Draw a person," your child will respond by drawing a head and trunk, arms and legs, and shoulders.

Copies a circle. Show your child a circle without drawing it in front of her, then ask her to copy it.

49-60 Months

Cuts following a line. Draw a 2- or 3-inch rather thick line (a wide-tipped marker is perfect) on a piece of paper, and give your child a small rounded-end scissors. She cuts on or along the line when she has mastered this step.

Knows simple opposites. Ask your child, "What is the opposite of in ?" or say, "If it's not up, then it is . . . what?" or "If it's not light, then it must be . . . what?"

Knows about the seasons and related activities. Ask your child to talk about each of the seasons and note whether she can describe some activities that occur in each. For example, ask her to talk about winter, and note whether she is able to associate winter with cold, snow, or Christmas, and so forth.

Names at least four colors. Red, blue, green, and yellow are four colors your child might know.

Counts three objects by pointing. Reaching this milestone shows that your child is learning concepts beyond "one" of something. Simply place an array of objects or toys in front of your child, and ask her to point to three of them.

61-72 Months

Copies capital letters (O, V, H, and T). Show your child a piece of paper with these letters written on it. Ask her to copy them on the same paper, and note whether she makes a recognizable copy of each one.

Counts three to five fingers and tells how many. Hold up three fingers and ask your child, "How many is this?" Do the same with four and five fingers. She passes the milestone when she counts the fingers correctly.

Matches a printed number with objects. Show your child a printed number, then ask her to point to a group of objects of the same number.

Sorts objects by size, color, and shape. Place an assortment of toys and objects in front of your child. Tell her to give you all the "red" ones, or all the "little" ones, and so forth. Your child may even be able to identify objects that don't belong.

Points to named numbers. Name a number while showing your child a group of printed numbers, then ask her to point to the printed number that you named. You might also ask the child to find a named number for television viewing in a TV schedule or on a TV channel selector.

Adapting

0-4 Months

Eats regularly and waits to be fed. By this milestone your child has developed a regular schedule and waits to be fed.

Gets excited at feeding preparations. Your child starts to kick, squirm, or maybe even quiet when she notices you beginning to prepare for a feeding. She may recognize the sound of the refrigerator, or microwave, or see you get the bottle or spoon to feed her.

Shows awareness of strangers. At this step, your child notices things out of the ordinary, including people she does not see often. She may quiet, frown, stare intently, cry, or cling.

Feeds no more than once during the night. Your child is able to take in enough nourishment during the day to require only one feeding, if any, after she is put to bed for the night.

Responds to parent's presence. Your child quiets or excites when she sees, hears, or feels you.

5-8 Months

Eats baby food. Your baby is ready to begin eating pureed food at this stage. Eating semi-solid food is a step toward independence.

Feeds self finger foods. Check with your health care provider about finger foods that are safe for your self-feeding child.

Holds own bottle to drink. While your child might prefer you to hold her and the bottle, when she passes this milestone, she is able to hold it for herself.

Refuses things. Independence and adaptation to life include learning to refuse things or activities such as foods, toys, diapering, dressing, bathing, or face washing.

Shows attachment to parent. An important step to your child's confidence in herself and abilities is the security of knowing you are there and will come for her when she calls or will return when you leave. Her attachment to you now shows she relies on you to met her physical, emotional, mental, and social needs. Note that she is unhappy, cries, or fusses when you leave her.

9-12 Months

Holds cup to drink. Your child may use "sippy" cups and training cups and be very messy, but holds and tips the cup to drink by herself.

Occupies self for 10 minutes or longer. Your child's lengthening attention span is an important step in gaining independence. Note that she plays contentedly by herself without interruption for at least 10 minutes.

Cooperates during dressing. Pushing arms into sleeves, stepping into pants, and holding still while you tie shoes, shows your child's cooperation in dressing.

Holds a spoon at meal time. Your child may not actually use the spoon to eat, or may use it sporadically or messily, but she does hold it in relationship to eating.

Chooses toys deliberately. Your child clearly prefers some toys and refuses or ignores others.

13-16 Months

Brings things to an adult for fixing or for help. Your child comes to you with a problem she wants help with, or a toy that needs fixing, and asks for help.

Seats self in a chair for short periods of time. Your child chooses to sit down in a child- or adult-sized chair, a booster chair, a car seat, or a potty chair, and stays there for a few minutes.

Discards the bottle. Once on a complete well balanced diet of baby food, your child is ready (with your help) to discard her bottle.

Indicates wet or soiled diaper. Your child makes sounds, says words, or points to her diaper to tell you she needs a diaper change.

Makes wants known. Your child clearly and even forcefully lets you know what she wants by pointing, tugging, or verbalizing.

17-20 Months

Eats without help. This milestone is an important marker of your child's developing independence. She feeds herself with or without utensils, without your help.

Leads adults to things. The ability to communicate needs, wants, and ideas is an important step to your child's independence. This includes leading you to what she wants or sees.

Helps with dressing. This milestone differs from cooperating in dressing in that your child will actually help. She might get needed garments, partially put them on, or help to pull them up.

Puts on shoes. While her shoes might be on the wrong feet and need fastening, your child is able to put on her own shoes.

Zips and unzips. It is important to check your child's clothing for zippers that have larger pulls and that operate smoothly so that she masters this milestone. Your child may not be able to start a jacket zipper, but is able to pull it up and down.

21-24 Months

Asks for food or drink. Your child asks, in any manner, for food items and something to drink when she has developed enough independence.

Puts toys away with encouragement. Watch to see that your child follows your supervised toy clean up. Help your child focus on picking up a specific item or group of items and direct her where to put them, and then follow with praise.

Eats table food including cut meats. This milestone marks your child's ability to take, chew, and swallow bites of many of the foods you normally eat.

Shares attention. Your child is gaining independence by being able to do things without your full attention.

Turns knobs and opens doors. Your child is able to open most doors inward and outward.

25-30 Months

Puts on simple clothing. Your child dresses herself by putting on simple items like elastic waisted pants or skirts, loose-fitting shirts, or slip-on shoes.

Cooperates in washing hands. Taking this step does not require that your child be able to completely wash her hands without help, but simply be willing to participate in hand washing.

Asks to use the toilet. Using whatever words she has learned, your child asks or states her need to use the bathroom.

Cooperates in brushing teeth. While you may need to supervise and help in teeth brushing, your child helps with preparations, brushes in some manner, and allows you to quickly finish brushing.

Follows routines at meals, bedtime, etc. Established routines like hand-washing before meals, brushing teeth at bedtime, clearing dishes after meals, and gathering nap-time accessories are now a regular part of your child's day, and she recognizes and accepts these routines.

31-36 Months

Initiates purposeful, often brief conversations. Your child shares her experiences, discusses her plans, and states her wishes in brief conversations with you and others. She follows trains of thought in these dialogues and asks and answers related questions.

Is orderly. Your child puts some things away and straightens toys and other belongings on her own — an important step to your child's developing organization in her world.

Avoids danger. Your child doesn't step out into the street, doesn't touch hot things, doesn't walk in front of moving cars or bikes, and knows how to avoid most dangerous situations.

Takes turns. Your child waits her turn, knowing that she will get an opportunity to do something after someone else.

Shows clothing preferences. Your child picks out her own clothes to wear, and may even insist on the same outfit each day.

37-42 Months

Puts on own shoes, pants, and underwear. Your child puts on her own shoes, pants, and underwear, but shirts and jackets may still present a problem and she may need help with them.

Undresses. Your child completely disrobes, even pulling off tee shirts and untying shoes.

Feeds self neatly. Your child has finally mastered the art of eating without making too much of a mess — her food stays on the plate and makes it to her mouth, her milk is not spilled or drooled, and her face is fairly clean at the end of a meal.

Separates from parent with little fuss. While your child may not like your leaving, she will not cry or throw a tantrum when you do leave for a short while.

Focuses on a task without being distracted. You notice that your child becomes engrossed in an activity, that she is paying attention to detail and may not hear you talk or notice other activities going on nearby.

43-48 Months

Puts shoes on correct feet. Your child notices the difference between the left and right shoes, and she puts them on the correct feet or senses by sight or by feel when her shoes are on the wrong feet and corrects the situation.

Uses a fork and a spoon. Your child uses both a fork and a spoon successfully.

Uses the toilet without help. While your child might notify you that she needs to use the toilet, she does use it efficiently without your help.

Does one or more household chores. You will be able to assign your child at least one easy household job on a regular basis. Chores might include clearing dishes from the table, picking up food from the floor, setting the table, collecting dirty clothes, and so forth.

Helps with easy meals. Your child may get the bread and the peanut butter for sandwiches, stir the macaroni and cheese, put the cheese on the bread, or other similar meal preparation tasks.

49-60 Months

Washes own hands and face. You may have to tell her to wash her face and hands, but she does it well without your help.

Completely dresses self. She is now able to put on all articles of clothing on her own, including socks, underwear, shirt, pants, shoes, and jacket.

Asks for bathroom privacy. Your child is developing a sense of self when she realizes her need for privacy. She won't want you or anyone else in the bathroom, and she may close and even lock the door.

Pours liquid into a glass. Your child pours herself a glass of water, juice, or milk with little spilling.

Starts and finishes easy projects. Watch your child as she starts and completely finishes her projects like finishing a sewing card, straightening her room, organizing her toys, or building a tower.

61-72 Months

Goes to bed when told. While you tell your child when to go to bed, she gets ready and goes to bed willingly, without supervision.

Crosses the street safely. Your child crosses at corners, stopping and looking both ways before crossing the street. She may recognize crossing symbols and light signals for crossing.

Laces and ties shoes. Your child may not tie her shoes tightly, or as you would, but she can tie them.

Bathes or showers alone. Along with bathroom privacy comes your child's need to wash herself in privacy, and she will do an adequate job.

Brushes own teeth thoroughly. By this stage, your child completely and thoroughly cleans her own teeth.

Growing

0-4 Months

Weighs 10 to 18 pounds. Your health care provider will have more specific weight expectations for your child based on her birth weight.

Measures 23 to 27 inches. Your health care provider will have more specific length expectations for your child based on her length at birth.

Hears well — responds to a voice in a quiet setting. In a quiet room and from behind your child, say something. If she responds, her hearing is normal.

Has two of three DTP and polio vaccinations. DTP (diphtheria, tetanus, and pertussis) vaccine is usually administered as a single vaccination. Your health care provider will have a specific schedule for your child and may recommend additional tests and immunizations.

Sleeps a total of 11 to 18 hours. Two naps per day with a nighttime stretch of 8 to 14 hours per day are common to children in this age group. Your child may have a very different schedule, but probably needs a total of 11 to 18 hours of sleep per 24-hour period.

5-8 Months

Weighs 14 to 23 pounds. Your child gains weight proportionate to her height and based upon her previous weight.

Measures 25 to 30 inches. Your child grows in length proportionate to her weight gain and based upon her previous length.

Has third and final DTP vaccination. Your health care provider will have a specific schedule for your child and may recommend additional tests and immunizations.

Has two to four teeth. Your child's first tooth is probably one of her bottom front teeth.

Sleeps a total of 9 to 18 hours. Your child starts to sleep about 8 to 13 hours at night with two naps during the day per 24-hour period.

9-12 Months

Weighs 17 to 27 pounds. Your child gains weight proportionate to her height and based upon her previous weight.

Measures 27 to 32 inches. Your child grows in length proportionate to her weight gain and based upon her previous length.

Has five to seven teeth. Your child probably has all four of her front teeth by now.

Has tuberculin and hematocrit or hemoglobin tests. Your health care provider will have a specific schedule for your child and may recommend additional tests and immunizations.

Hears well — responds to a voice in a quiet setting. In a quiet room and from behind your child, say something she is sure to respond to. If she responds, her hearing is normal.

13-16 Months

Weighs 17 to 29 pounds. Your child gains weight proportionate to her height and based upon her previous weight

Measures 27 to 33 inches. Your child grows in length proportionate to her weight gain and based upon her previous length.

Has eight to ten teeth. Your child continues to cut teeth and at this milestone has all eight (four on top and four on the bottom) of her front teeth.

Has measles, mumps, and rubella vaccinations. Health care providers frequently refer to these as MMR and will have a specific schedule for your child.

Sleeps a total of 9 to 12 hours. Your child's sleep requirements lessen, leaving her more time to play and learn.

17-20 Months

Weighs 18 to 32 pounds. Your child gains weight proportionate to her height and based upon her previous weight.

Measures 29 to 36 inches. Your child grows in length proportionate to her weight gain and based upon her previous length.

Has 11 to 15 teeth. By this milestone your child has a molar or two.

Has DTP booster and final polio vaccination. Your health care provider will have a specific schedule for your child and may recommend additional tests and immunizations.

Hears well — responds to a voice in a quiet setting. In a quiet room and from behind your child, say something she is sure to respond to. If she responds, her hearing is normal.

21-24 Months

Weighs 21 to 33 pounds. Your child gains weight proportionate to her height and based upon her previous weight.

Measures 31 to 37 inches. Your child grows in height proportionate to her weight gain and based upon her previous height.

Has 16 to 18 teeth. Your child has all eight front teeth, four molars and some cuspids (eye teeth).

Has influenza (Hib, or *Haemophilus influenzae* type B) immunization. Your health care provider will have a specific schedule for your child and may recommend additional tests and immunizations.

Sleeps a total of 9 to 12 hours. An afternoon nap is probably needed with the remainder of needed sleep occurring at night.

25-30 Months

Weighs 22 to 35 pounds. Your child gains weight proportionate to her height and based upon her previous weight.

Measures 32 to 39 inches. Your child grows in height proportionate to her weight gain and based upon her previous height.

Has a dry diaper after napping. This may be your first indication that your child's urination and bowel movements are becoming voluntary and can be self-controlled. Your child may be able to hold her urine for up to an hour and a half.

Has 18 to 20 teeth. Your child's teeth include all eight front teeth, four to eight molars, and one to four cuspids or eye teeth.

Hears well — responds to directions. Give your child a few easy directions that are fun and rewarding, like "Run to the post and back" or "Go get yourself a treat." If she responds, even to refuse or argue, she has passed this milestone.

31-36 Months

Weighs 24 to 38 pounds. Your child gains weight proportionate to her height and based upon her previous weight.

Measures 34 to 41 inches. Your child grows in height proportionate to her weight gain and based upon her previous height.

Sleeps a total of 9 to 12 hours. An afternoon nap may be needed, but most sleep occurs at night.

Has dental examination. Most dentists recommend that your child's first dental exam occur after she has all 20 of her baby teeth, then regularly and at least yearly thereafter.

Has 20 teeth. This milestone marks the completion of your child's first teeth.

37-42 Months

Weighs 25 to 40 pounds. Your child gains weight proportionate to her height and based upon her previous weight.

Measures 35 to 42 inches. Your child grows in height proportionate to her weight gain and based upon her previous height.

Legs lengthen and stomach flattens. Your child looks a little leaner and has a straighter posture by this milestone.

Hears well — responds to a whisper. In a quiet room and from behind your child, whisper something she is sure to respond to. If she responds, her hearing is normal.

Sees well. Assuming that you have good (even if lens-corrected) vision, determine if your child is able to see things that you can see at varying distances; if she can, she passes this step.

43-48 Months

Weighs 27 to 43 pounds. Your child gains weight proportionate to her height and based upon her previous weight.

Measures 36 to 44 inches. Your child grows in height proportionate to her weight gain and based upon her previous height.

Naps briefly or not at all. Your child may still need a quiet rest period. She may nap one day and not the next and/or nap briefly.

Sleeps a total of 9 to 12 hours. A child passing this milestone is making more of her daylight hours by doing most of her sleeping at night.

Has the proportions of a child rather than a toddler. Your child appears leaner, with her head and body proportions more like that of a miniature adult.

49-60 Months

Weighs 30 to 50 pounds. Your child gains weight proportionate to her height and based upon her previous weight.

Measures 38 to 46 inches. Your child grows in height proportionate to her weight gain and based upon her previous height.

Has had DTP and polio booster shots. Your health care provider will have a specific schedule for your child and may recommend additional tests and immunizations.

Passes hearing screening. Hearing screenings are usually done during the child's first year in school—ask for the results.

Responds to standard "E" chart eye test. This is a vision screening test, the first formal vision test your child may have. It is usually given during the child's first year in school — ask for the results.

61-72 Months

Weighs 33 to 57 pounds. Your child gains weight proportionate to her height and based upon her previous weight.

Measures 42 to 49 inches. Your child grows in height proportionate to her weight gain and based upon her previous height.

Feet have arches and legs are straight. While your child may not develop arches because of heredity, if she is going to, it will happen now. Her legs should have lost most of their bowing, although a little "toeing in" is normal and will not cause a problem.

Has fewer colds and flu. Your child builds up immunities to colds and flu with increased exposure to larger groups of children.

Passes scoliosis/posture screening. This is a routine screening test usually performed by your health care provider or school nurse — ask for the results.

References

Alpern, B. and Boll, T. Developmental Profile. Aspen, CO: Psychological Development Publications, 1972.

Bangs, T. Birth to Three. Allen, TX: Developmental Learning Materials, 1987.

Barnes, M., Crutchfield, C. and Heriza, C. The Neurophysiology Basis of Patient Treatment. Morgantown, WV: Stokesville Publishing Company, 1978.

Bayley, N. Bayley Infant Scales of Development. New York: Psychological Corporation, 1968.

Bower, T.G.R. Development in Infancy. San Francisco: W.H. Freeman & Company, 1974.

Brazelton, T.B. Touch Points: Your Child's Emotional and Behavioral Development. Reading, MA: Addison-Wesley Publishing Company, 1992.

Brazelton, T.B. The Neonatal Behavioral Assessment Scale. Philadelphia: J.B. Lippincott Company, 1973.

Bruner, J.S. Eye, Hand, and Mind. In D. Elkind and J.H. Flavell (Eds.) Studies in Cognitive Development: Essays in Honor of Jean Piaget. New York: Oxford University Press, 1969.

Caplan, F. The First Twelve Months of Life. New York: Bantam Books, 1971.

Caplan, F. and Caplan, T. The Early Childhood Years: The 2 to 6 Year Old. New York: Bantam Books, 1984.

Caplan, F. and Caplan, T. The Second Twelve Months of Life. New York: Bantam Books, 1980.

Cattell, P. The Measurement of Intelligence in Infants and Young Children. New York: Psychological Corporation, 1940.

Charlesworth, W.R. Development of the Object Concept: A Methodological Study. Paper presented at the meetings of the American Psychological Association, New York, 1969.

Cohen, M.A. and Gross, P.J. The Developmental Resource, Vol. I. New York: Grune & Stratton, 1979.

Doll, E. Preschool Attainment Record. Circle Pines, MN: American Guidance Service, 1966.

Doll, E. The Measurement of Social Competence: A Manual for the Vineland Social Maturity Scale. Circle Pines, MN: American Guidance Service, 1966.

Frankenberg, W. and Dodds, J. Denver Developmental Screening Test. Denver: Ladoca Project and Publishing Foundation, 1966.

Gesell, A. The First Five Years of Life: A Guide to the Study of the Preschool Child. New York: Harper, 1940.

Goodenough, F., Mauer, K. and Van Wagen, M. Minnesota Preschool Scale. Circle Pines, MN: American Guidance Service, 1940.

Hurlock, E. Child Growth and Development. New York: McGraw-Hill, Inc., 1968.

Joint Commission on Mental Health of Children. Mental Health of Children: Services, Research, and Manpower. New York: Harper & Row, Inc., 1973.

Kephart, N. The slow learner in the classroom. Columbus, OH: Charles E. Merrill, 1971.

Kiester, E. Jr., and Kiester, S.V. New Baby Book. Des Moines, IA: Better Homes & Gardens Books, 1985.

Kiester, E. Jr., (Ed.). New Family Medical Guide. Des Moines, IA: Better Homes & Gardens Books, 1982.

Koppitz, E. Bender-Gestalt Test for Young Children—Koppitz Method. New York: Grune & Stratton, 1964.

Kuhlman, F. A Handbook of Mental Tests: A Further Revision of the Binet-Simon Scale. Baltimore: Warwick & York, 1922.

Leach, P. Your Baby & Child, From Birth to Age Five. New York: Alfred A. Knopf, 1988.

Lowe, M. Trends in the development of representational play in infants from one to three years: An observational study. Journal of Child Psychology, 16: 33-48, 1975.

Lutterjohann, M. I.Q Tests for Children. Briarcliff Manor, NY: Stein & Day/Scarborough House, 1978.

Meier, J.H. SOL Facilitator's Handbook I, Foundations and Rationale: System for Open Learning. Denver: John H. Meier, 1970.

Miller, D.J., Cohen, L.B. and Hill, K.T. A methodological investigation of Piaget's theory of object concept development in the sensory-motor period. Journal of Experimental Child Psychology, 9: 59-85, 1970.

Newborg, J., Stock, J.R., Wnek, L., Guidibaldi, J. and Svinicki, J. Battelle Developmental Inventory. Allen, TX: Developmental Learning Materials, 1984.

Northern, J.L. and Downs, M.P. Hearing in Children. Baltimore: Williams & Wilkins Company, 1974.

Sanford, A. Learning Accomplishment Profile. Chapel Hill, NC: University of North Carolina at Chapel Hill, Chapel Hill Training — Outreach Project.

Schofield L. and Uzgiris, I.E. Examining Behavior and the Development of the Concept of the Object. Paper presented at the meetings of the Society for Research in Child Development. Santa Monica, CA, 1969.

Sheridan, M. The Developmental Progress of Infants and Young Children. London: Her Majesty's Stationery Office, 1968.

Slosson, R. Slosson Intelligence Test. New York: Slosson Educational Publishing, 1964.

Stot, D., Moyes, F and Henderson, S. Test of Motor Impairment (5th Edition). Toronto: Brook Educational Publishing, 1972.

Stutsman, R. Mental Measurement of the Preschool Child, A Guide for the Administration of the Merrill-Palmer Scale of Mental Test. Yonkers-on-Hudson, NY: World, 1931.

Uzgiris, I. and Hunt, J. Assessment in infancy: Ordinal Scales of Psychological Development. Urbana: University of Illinois Press, 1975.

White, B.L. Human Infants; Experience and Psychological Development. Englewood Cliffs, NJ: Prentice-Hall, 1971.

White, B.L. and Held, R. Experience in Early Human Development. Part 2: Plasticity of Sensorimotor Development in the Human Infant. In Exceptional Infant, Vol. 1. Seattle: Special Child Publications, 1967.

Index

Notes

Notes